MW01057180

Introduction

Mathematical Thinking in Kindergarten

Kindergarten

Karen Economopoulos
Megan Murray

Developed at TERC, Cambridge, Massachusetts

Dale Seymour Publications®
White Plains, New York

The *Investigations* curriculum was developed at TERC (formerly Technical Education Research Centers) in collaboration with Kent State University and the State University of New York at Buffalo. The work was supported in part by National Science Foundation Grant No. ESI-9050210. TERC is a nonprofit company working to improve mathematics and science education. TERC is located at 2067 Massachusetts Avenue, Cambridge, MA 02140.

This project was supported, in part,
by the
National Science Foundation
Opinions expressed are those of the authors
and not necessarily those of the Foundation

Managing Editor: Catherine Anderson
Series Editor: Beverly Cory
ESL Consultant: Nancy Sokol Green
Production/Manufacturing Director: Janet Yearian
Production/Manufacturing Manager: Karen Edmonds
Production/Manufacturing Coordinators: Joe Conte, Roxanne Knoll
Design Manager: Jeff Kelly
Design: Don Taka
Composition: Archetype Book Composition
Illustrations: DJ Simison, Rachel Gage, Carl Yoshihara
Cover: Bay Graphics

This book is published by Dale Seymour Publications®, an imprint of Addison Wesley Longman, Inc.

Dale Seymour Publications
10 Bank Street
White Plains, NY 10602
Customer Service: 1-800-872-1100

Copyright © 1998 by Dale Seymour Publications®. All rights reserved. Printed in the United States of America.

Limited reproduction permission: The publisher grants permission to individual teachers who have purchased this book to reproduce the blackline masters as needed for use with their own students. Reproduction for an entire school or school district or for commercial use is prohibited.

Order number DS47103
ISBN 1-57232-926-2
4 5 6 7 8 9 10-ML-02 01 00 99

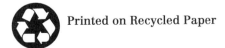 Printed on Recycled Paper

T E R C

INVESTIGATIONS IN NUMBER, DATA, AND SPACE®

Principal Investigator   Susan Jo Russell

Co-Principal Investigator   Cornelia Tierney

Director of Research and Evaluation   Jan Mokros

Director of K–2 Curriculum   Karen Economopoulos

Curriculum Development
Karen Economopoulos
Rebeka Eston
Marlene Kliman
Christopher Mainhart
Jan Mokros
Megan Murray
Kim O'Neil
Susan Jo Russell
Tracey Wright

Evaluation and Assessment
Mary Berle-Carman
Jan Mokros
Andee Rubin

Teacher Support
Irene Baker
Megan Murray
Kim O'Neil
Judy Storeygard
Tracey Wright

Technology Development
Michael T. Battista
Douglas H. Clements
Julie Sarama

Video Production
David A. Smith
Judy Storeygard

Administration and Production
Irene Baker
Amy Catlin

**Cooperating Classrooms
for This Unit**
Jeanne Wall
Arlington Public Schools
Arlington, MA

Audrey Barzey
Patricia Kelliher
Ellen Tait
Boston Public Schools
Boston, MA

Meg Bruton
Fayerweather Street School
Cambridge, MA

Rebeka Eston
Lincoln Public Schools
Lincoln, MA

Lila Austin
The Atrium School
Watertown, MA

Christopher Mainhart
Westwood Public Schools
Westwood, MA

Consultants and Advisors
Deborah Lowenberg Ball
Michael T. Battista
Marilyn Burns
Douglas H. Clements
Ann Grady

CONTENTS

WHERE TO START

The first-time user of *Mathematical Thinking in Kindergarten* should read the following:

When you next teach this same unit, you can begin to read more of the background. Each time you present the unit, you will learn more about how your students understand the mathematical ideas.

Investigations in Number, Data, and Space® is a K–5 mathematics curriculum with four major goals:

- to offer students meaningful mathematical problems
- to emphasize depth in mathematical thinking rather than superficial exposure to a series of fragmented topics
- to communicate mathematics content and pedagogy to teachers
- to substantially expand the pool of mathematically literate students

The *Investigations* curriculum embodies a new approach based on years of research about how children learn mathematics. Each grade level consists of a set of separate units, each offering 2–8 weeks of work. These units of study are presented through investigations that involve students in the exploration of major mathematical ideas.

Approaching the mathematics content through investigations helps students develop flexibility and confidence in approaching problems, fluency in using mathematical skills and tools to solve problems, and proficiency in evaluating their solutions. Students also build a repertoire of ways to communicate about their mathematical thinking, while their enjoyment and appreciation of mathematics grows.

The investigations are carefully designed to invite all students into mathematics—girls and boys, members of diverse cultural, ethnic, and language groups, and students with different strengths and interests. Problem contexts often call on students to share experiences from their family, culture, or community. The curriculum eliminates barriers—such as work in isolation from peers, or emphasis on speed and memorization—that exclude some students from participating successfully in mathematics. The following aspects of the curriculum ensure that all students are included in significant mathematics learning:

- Students spend time exploring problems in depth.
- They find more than one solution to many of the problems they work on.
- They invent their own strategies and approaches, rather than rely on memorized procedures.
- They choose from a variety of concrete materials and appropriate technology, including calculators, as a natural part of their everyday mathematical work.
- They express their mathematical thinking through drawing, writing, and talking.
- They work in a variety of groupings—as a whole class, individually, in pairs, and in small groups.
- They move around the classroom as they explore the mathematics in their environment and talk with their peers.

While reading and other language activities are typically given a great deal of time and emphasis in elementary classrooms, mathematics often does not get the time it needs. If students are to experience mathematics in depth, they must have enough time to become engaged in real mathematical problems. We believe that a minimum of 5 hours of mathematics classroom time a week—about an hour a day—is critical at the elementary level. The scope and pacing of the *Investigations* curriculum are based on that belief.

We explain more about the pedagogy and principles that underlie these investigations in Teacher Notes throughout the units. For correlations of the curriculum to the NCTM Standards and further help in using this research-based program for teaching mathematics, see the following books, available from Dale Seymour Publications:

- *Implementing the* Investigations in Number, Data, and Space® *Curriculum*
- *Beyond Arithmetic: Changing Mathematics in the Elementary Classroom* by Jan Mokros, Susan Jo Russell, and Karen Economopoulos

This book is one of the curriculum units for *Investigations in Number, Data, and Space.* In addition to providing part of a complete mathematics curriculum for your students, this unit offers information to support your own professional development. You, the teacher, are the person who will make this curriculum come alive in the classroom; the book for each unit is your main support system.

Although the curriculum does not include student instructional texts, reproducible sheets for student work are provided with the units and, in some cases, are also available as Student Activity Booklets. In these investigations, students work actively with objects and experiences in their own environment, including manipulative materials and technology, rather than with a workbook.

Ultimately, every teacher will use these investigations in ways that make sense for his or her particular style, the particular group of students, and the constraints and supports of a particular school environment. Each unit offers information and guidance drawn from our collaborations with many teachers and students over many years. Our goal is to help you, a professional educator, give all your students access to mathematical power.

Investigation Format

The opening two pages of each investigation help you get ready for the work that follows.

- **Focus Time** This gives a synopsis of the activities used to introduce the important mathematical ideas for the investigation.
- **Choice Time** This lists the activities, new and recurring, that support the Focus Time work.
- **Mathematical Emphasis** This highlights the most important ideas and processes students will encounter in this investigation.
- **Teacher Support** This indicates the Teacher Notes and Dialogue Boxes included to help you understand what's going on mathematically in your classroom.
- **What to Plan Ahead of Time** These lists alert you to materials to gather, sheets to duplicate, and other things you need to do before starting the investigation. Full details of materials and preparation are included with each activity.

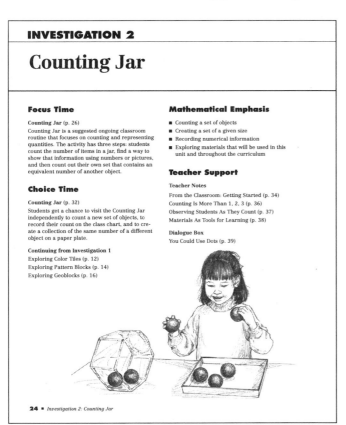

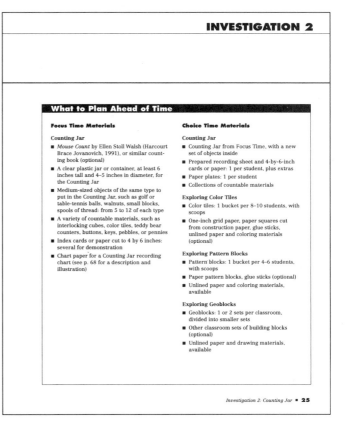

Always read through an entire investigation before you begin, in order to understand the overall flow and sequence of the activities.

Focus Time In this whole-group meeting, you introduce one or more activities that embody the important mathematical ideas underlying the investigation. The group then may break up into individuals or pairs for further work on the same activity. Many Focus Time activities culminate with a brief sharing time or discussion as a way of acknowledging students' work and highlighting the mathematical ideas. Focus Time varies in length. Sometimes it is short and can be completed in a single group meeting or a single work period; other times it may stretch over two or three sessions.

Choice Time Each Focus Time is followed by Choice Time, which offers a series of supporting activities to be done simultaneously by individuals, pairs, or small groups. You introduce these related tasks over a period of several days. During Choice Time, students work independently, at their own pace, choosing the activities they prefer and often returning many times to their favorites. Many kindergarten classrooms have an activity time built into their daily schedule, and Choice Time activities can easily be incorporated.

Together, the Focus Time and Choice Time activities offer a balanced kindergarten curriculum.

Classroom Routines The kindergarten day is filled with opportunities to work with mathematics. Routines such as taking attendance, asking about snack preferences, and discussing the calendar offer regular, ongoing practice in counting, collecting and organizing data, and understanding time.

Four specific routines—Attendance, Counting Jar, Calendar, and Today's Question—are formally introduced in the unit *Mathematical Thinking in Kindergarten*. Another routine, Patterns on the Pocket Chart, is introduced in the unit *Pattern Trains and Hopscotch Paths*. Descriptions of these routines can also be found in an appendix for each unit, and reminders of their ongoing use appear in the Unit Overview charts.

The Linguistically Diverse Classroom Each unit includes an appendix with Tips for the Linguistically Diverse Classroom to help teachers support stu-

dents at varying levels of English proficiency. While more specific tips appear within the units at grades 1–5, often in relation to written work, general tips on oral discussions and observing the students are more appropriate for kindergarten.

Also included are suggestions for vocabulary work to help ensure that students' linguistic difficulties do not interfere with their comprehension of math concepts. The Preview for the Linguistically Diverse Classroom lists key words in the unit that are generally known to English-speaking kindergartners. Activities to help familiarize other students with these words are found in the appendix, Vocabulary Support for Second-Language Learners. In addition, ideas for making connections to students' languages and cultures, included on the Preview page, help the class explore the unit's concepts from a multicultural perspective.

Materials

A complete list of the materials needed for teaching this unit follows the Unit Overview. These materials are available in *Investigations* kits or can be purchased from school supply dealers.

Classroom Materials In an active kindergarten mathematics classroom, certain basic materials should be available at all times, including interlocking cubes, a variety of things to count with, and writing and drawing materials. Some activities in this curriculum require scissors and glue sticks or tape; dot stickers and large paper are also useful. So that students can independently get what they need at any time, they should know where the materials are kept, how they are stored, and how they are to be returned to the storage area.

Children's Literature Each unit offers a list of children's literature that can be used to support the mathematical ideas in the unit. Sometimes an activity incorporates a specific children's book, with suggestions for substitutions where practical. While such activities can be adapted and taught without the book, the literature offers a rich introduction and should be used whenever possible. If you can get the titles in Big Book format, these are ideal for kindergarten.

Blackline Masters Student recording sheets and other teaching tools for both class and homework are provided as reproducible blackline masters at the end of each unit. When student sheets are designated for kindergarten homework, they usually repeat an activity from class, such as playing a game, as a way of involving and informing family members. Occasionally a homework sheet may ask students to collect data or materials for a class project or in preparation for upcoming activities.

Student Activity Booklets For the two kindergarten number units, the blackline masters are also available as Student Activity Booklets, designed to free you from extensive copying. The other kindergarten units require minimal copying.

Family Letter A letter that you can send home to students' families is included with the blackline masters for each unit. Families need to be informed about the mathematics work in your classroom; they should be encouraged to participate in and support their children's work. A reminder to send home the letter for each unit appears in one of the early investigations. These letters are also available separately in Spanish, Vietnamese, Cantonese, Hmong, and Cambodian.

***Investigations* at Home** To further involve families in the kindergarten program, you can offer them the *Investigations* at Home booklet, which describes the kindergarten units, explains the mathematics work children do in kindergarten, and offers activities families can do with their children at home.

Adapting *Investigations* to Your Classroom

Kindergarten programs vary greatly in the amount of time each day that students attend. We recommend that kindergarten teachers devote from 30 to 45 minutes daily to work in mathematics, but we recognize that this can be challenging in a half-day program. The kindergarten level of *Investigations* is intentionally flexible so that teachers can adapt the curriculum to their particular setup.

Kindergartens participating in the *Investigations* field test included full-day programs, half-day programs of approximately 3 hours, and half-day programs that add one or two full days to the kindergarten week at some point in the school year. Despite the wide range of program structures, classrooms generally fell into one of two

groups: those that offered a separate math time daily (Math Workshop or Math Time), and those that included one or two mathematics activities during a general Activity Time or Station Time.

Math Workshop Teachers using a Math Workshop approach set aside 30 to 45 minutes each day for doing mathematics. In addition, they usually also have a more general activity time in their daily schedule. On some days, Math Workshop might be devoted to the Focus Time activities, with the whole class gathered together. On other days, students might work in small groups and choose from three or four Choice Time activities.

Math as Part of Activity Time Teachers with less time in their day may offer students one or two math activities, along with activities from other areas of the curriculum, during their Activity Time or Station Time. For example, on a particular day, students might be able to choose among a science activity, block building, an art project, dramatic play, books, puzzles, and a math activity. New activities are introduced during a whole-class meeting. With the *Investigations* curriculum, teachers who use this approach have found that it is important to designate at least one longer block of time (30 to 45 minutes) each week for mathematics. During this time, students engage in Focus Time activities and have a chance to share their work and discuss mathematical ideas. The suggested Choice Time activities are then presented as part of the general activity time. Following this model, work on a curriculum unit will naturally stretch over a longer period.

Planning Your Curriculum The amount of time scheduled for mathematics work will determine how much of the kindergarten *Investigations* curriculum a teacher is able to cover in the school year. You may have to make some choices as you adapt the units to your particular schedule. What is most important is finding a way to involve students in mathematics every day of the school year.

Each unit will be handled somewhat differently by every teacher. You need to be active in determining an appropriate pace and the best transition points for your class. As you read an investigation, make some preliminary decisions about how many days you will need to present the activities, based on what you know about your students and about your schedule. You may need to modify your initial plans as you proceed, and you may want to make notes in the margins of the pages as reminders for the next time you use the unit.

Help for You, the Teacher

Because we believe strongly that a new curriculum must help teachers think in new ways about mathematics and about their students' mathematical thinking processes, we have included a great deal of material to help you learn more about both.

About the Mathematics in This Unit This introductory section summarizes the essential information about the mathematics you will be teaching. It describes the unit's central mathematical ideas and the ways students will encounter them through the unit's activities.

Teacher Notes These reference notes provide practical information about the mathematics you are teaching and about our experience with how students learn. Many of the notes were written in response to actual questions from teachers or to discuss important things we saw happening in the field-test classrooms. Some teachers like to read them all before starting the unit, then review them as they come up in particular investigations.

In the kindergarten units, Teacher Notes headed "From the Classroom" contain anecdotal reflections of teachers. Some focus on classroom management issues, while others are observations of students at work. These notes offer another perspective on how an activity might unfold or how kindergarten students might become engaged with a particular material or activity.

A few Teacher Notes touch on fundamental principles of using *Investigations* and focus on the pedagogy of the kindergarten classroom:

- About Choice Time
- Materials as Tools for Learning
- Encouraging Students to Think, Reason, and Share Ideas
- Games: The Importance of Playing More Than Once

After their initial appearance, these are repeated in the back of each unit. Reviewing these notes periodically can help you reflect on important aspects of the *Investigations* curriculum.

Dialogue Boxes Sample dialogues demonstrate how students typically express their mathematical ideas, what issues and confusions arise in their thinking, and how some teachers have guided class discussions.

Many of these dialogues are word-for-word transcriptions of recorded class discussions. They are not always easy reading; sometimes it may take some effort to unravel what the students are trying to say. But this is the value of these dialogues; they offer good clues to how your students may develop and express their approaches and strategies, helping you prepare for your own class discussions.

Where to Start You may not have time to read everything the first time you use this unit. As a first-time user, you will likely focus on understanding the activities and working them out with your students. You will also want to read the few sections listed in the Contents under the heading Where to Start.

Flowers, Dancers, and Pattern Block Walls

Students vary in the amount of structure and direction they need as they freely explore materials. Asking questions can be an effective way of guiding and structuring a free exploration experience for some students. This can extend their thinking about a particular material and lead them into new ways of using it. When students work with a partner or small group, they benefit from observing how others use materials. Inviting students to share their constructions and designs is a natural way to exchange ideas.

The following dialogue occurred early in the year during a free exploration Choice Time. The teacher joins a small group of students working with pattern blocks and asks them to tell her about their constructions.

Kylie: I have a flower. See, the yellow one is the middle, and then the flower part is all around with the blue. And then the green triangles are the stem part.

Gabriela: Mine is a person. Here is her hat. It's red. And then she sort of looks like she is dancing, because these ones, these blue diamonds are her legs.

Yes, you made her legs using the blue rhombus shapes, and it does look like she is dancing.

Kylie: And you used green triangles just like me. But you made her arms and I made a stem.

Carlo: Stop shaking the table! I don't want my wall to fall down.

Some of you have decided to use the pattern blocks flat on the table and some of you have used them to build up, sort of like blocks. It is harder to keep them in place when they're on their edges the way Carlo has them. Carlo, can you tell me about your wall?

Carlo: Well, it goes yellow, red, yellow, red, yellow, red and then it switches to yellow, blue, yellow, blue. See, they sort of fit together, right next to each other.

Yes, I see that the side of the red trapezoid fits right into the side of the yellow hexagon. And the side of the blue rhombus also fits into the side of the hexagon. I wonder what other blocks will fit exactly together so that you can make that kind of wall?

The conversation is interrupted by some commotion at another table. Three students are building elaborate constructions using pattern blocks. Two are being silly, sliding blocks back and forth across the table. The teacher addresses these two students.

Ravi and Tess, I remember that the other day you were interested in trying to make a design that would cover a piece of drawing paper, but time ran out and you didn't have a chance to do it. Would you be interested in trying to work on that problem now?

Ravi: Yeah, let's do that.

Tess: No, I don't want to. I want to keep doing this. *[She slides another block across the table.]*

Ravi, you can get a piece of paper from the art shelf. Tess, you'll have to make a choice about what you want to do. Sliding blocks is not one of the choices of how to use the pattern blocks. If you want to use the blocks today, you'll have to use them in a responsible way. If not, you'll need to leave this activity and make a new choice.

The *Investigations* curriculum incorporates the use of two forms of technology in the classroom: calculators and computers. Calculators are assumed to be standard classroom materials, available for student use in any unit. Computers are explicitly linked to one or more units at each grade level; they are used with the unit on 2-D geometry at each grade, as well as with some of the units on measuring, data, and changes.

Using Calculators

In this curriculum, calculators are considered tools for doing mathematics, similar to pattern blocks or interlocking cubes. Just as with other tools, students must learn both *how* to use calculators correctly and *when* they are appropriate to use. This knowledge is crucial for daily life, as calculators are now a standard way of handling numerical operations, both at work and at home. Calculators are formally introduced in the grade 1 curriculum, but if available, can be introduced to kindergartners informally.

Using a calculator correctly is not a simple task; it depends on a good knowledge of the four operations and of the number system, so that students can select suitable calculations and also determine what a reasonable result would be. These skills are the basis of any work with numbers, whether or not a calculator is involved.

Unfortunately, calculators are often seen as tools to check computations with, as if other methods are somehow more fallible. Students need to understand that any computational method can be used to check any other; it's just as easy to make a mistake on the calculator as it is to make a mistake on paper or with mental arithmetic. Throughout this curriculum, we encourage students to solve computation problems in more than one way in order to double-check their accuracy. We present mental arithmetic, paper-and-pencil computation, and calculators as three possible approaches.

In this curriculum we also recognize that, despite their importance, calculators are not always appropriate in mathematics instruction. Like any tools, calculators are useful for some tasks but not for others. You will need to make decisions about when to allow students access to calculators and when to ask that they solve problems without them, so that they can concentrate on other tools and skills. At times when calculators are or are not appropriate for a particular activity, we make specific recommendations. Help your students develop their own sense of which problems they can tackle with their own reasoning and which ones might be better solved with a combination of their own reasoning and the calculator.

Managing calculators in your classroom so that they are a tool, and not a distraction, requires some planning. When calculators are first introduced, students often want to use them for everything, even problems that can be solved quite simply by other methods. However, once the novelty wears off, students are just as interested in developing their own strategies, especially when these strategies are emphasized and valued in the classroom. Over time, students will come to recognize the ease and value of solving problems mentally, with paper and pencil, or with manipulatives, while also understanding the power of the calculator to facilitate work with larger numbers.

Experience shows that if calculators are available only occasionally, students become excited and distracted when permitted to use them. They focus on the tool rather than on the mathematics. In order to learn when calculators are appropriate and when they are not, students must have easy access to them and use them routinely in their work.

If you have a calculator for each student, and if you think your students can accept the responsibility, you might allow them to keep their calculators with the rest of their individual materials, at least for the first few weeks of school. Alternatively, you might store them in boxes on a shelf, number each calculator, and assign a corresponding number to each student. This system can give students a sense of ownership while also helping you keep track of the calculators.

Using Computers

Students can use computers to approach and visualize mathematical situations in new ways. The computer allows students to construct and manipulate geometric shapes, see objects move according to rules they specify, and turn, flip, and repeat a pattern.

This curriculum calls for computers in units where they are a particularly effective tool for learning mathematics content. One unit on 2-D geometry at each of the grades 3–5 includes a core of activities that rely on access to computers, either in the classroom or in a lab. Other units on geometry, measurement, data, and changes include computer activities, but can be taught without them. In these units, however, students' experience is greatly enhanced by computer use.

The following list outlines the recommended use of computers in this curriculum:

Kindergarten
Unit: *Making Shapes and Building Blocks*
   (Exploring Geometry)
Software: *Shapes*
Source: provided with the unit

Grade 1
Unit: *Survey Questions and Secret Rules*
   (Collecting and Sorting Data)
Software: *Tabletop, Jr.*
Source: Broderbund

Unit: *Quilt Squares and Block Towns*
   (2-D and 3-D Geometry)
Software: *Shapes*
Source: provided with the unit

Grade 2
Unit: *Mathematical Thinking at Grade 2*
   (Introduction)
Software: *Shapes*
Source: provided with the unit

Unit: *Shapes, Halves, and Symmetry*
   (Geometry and Fractions)
Software: *Shapes*
Source: provided with the unit

Unit: *How Long? How Far?* (Measuring)
Software: *Geo-Logo*
Source: provided with the unit

Grade 3
Unit: *Flips, Turns, and Area* (2-D Geometry)
Software: *Tumbling Tetrominoes*
Source: provided with the unit

Unit: *Turtle Paths* (2-D Geometry)
Software: *Geo-Logo*
Source: provided with the unit

Grade 4
Unit: *Sunken Ships and Grid Patterns*
   (2-D Geometry)
Software: *Geo-Logo*
Source: provided with the unit

Grade 5
Unit: *Picturing Polygons* (2-D Geometry)
Software: *Geo-Logo*
Source: provided with the unit

Unit: *Patterns of Change* (Tables and Graphs)
Software: *Trips*
Source: provided with the unit

Unit: *Data: Kids, Cats, and Ads* (Statistics)
Software: *Tabletop, Sr.*
Source: Broderbund

The software provided with the *Investigations* units uses the power of the computer to help students explore mathematical ideas and relationships that cannot be explored in the same way with physical materials. With the *Shapes* (grades K–2) and *Tumbling Tetrominoes* (grade 3) software, students explore symmetry, pattern, rotation and reflection, area, and characteristics of 2-D shapes. With the *Geo-Logo* software (grades 2–5), students investigate rotations and reflections, coordinate geometry, the properties of 2-D shapes, and angles. The *Trips* software (grade 5) is a mathematical exploration of motion in which students run experiments and interpret data presented in graphs and tables.

We suggest that students work in pairs on the computer; this not only maximizes computer resources but also encourages students to consult, monitor, and teach one another. However, asking more than two students to work at the same computer is less effective. Managing access to computers is an issue for every classroom. The curriculum gives you explicit support for setting up a system. The units are structured on the assumption that you have enough computers for half your students to work on the machines in pairs at one time. If you do not have access to that many computers, suggestions are made for structuring class time to use the unit with fewer than five.

Assessment plays a critical role in teaching and learning, and it is an integral part of the *Investigations* curriculum. For a teacher using these units, assessment is an ongoing process. You observe students' discussions and explanations of their ideas and strategies on a daily basis and examine their work as it evolves. While students are busy working with materials, playing mathematical games, sharing ideas with partners, and working on projects, you have many opportunities to observe their mathematical thinking. What you learn through observation guides your decisions about how to proceed, both with the curriculum and with individual students.

Our experiences with young children suggest that they know, can explain, and can demonstrate with materials a lot more than they can represent on paper. This is one reason why it is so important to engage children in conversation, helping them explain their thinking about a problem they are solving. It is also why, in kindergarten, assessment is based exclusively on a teacher's observations of students as they work.

The way you observe students will vary throughout the year. At times you may be interested in particular strategies that students are developing to solve problems. Other times, you might want to observe how students use or do not use materials for solving problems. You may want to focus on how students interact when working in pairs or groups. You may be interested in noting the strategy that a student uses when playing a game during Choice Time. Or you may take note of student ideas and thinking during class discussions.

Assessment Tools in the Unit

Virtually every activity in the kindergarten units of the *Investigations* curriculum includes a section called Observing the Students. This section is a teacher's primary assessment tool. It offers guidelines on what to look for as students encounter the mathematics of the activity. It may suggest questions you can ask to uncover student thinking or to stimulate further investigation. When useful, a range of potential responses or examples of typical student approaches are given, along with ways to adapt the activity for students in need of more or less challenge.

Supplementing this main assessment tool in each unit are the Teacher Notes and Dialogue Boxes that contain examples of student work, teacher observations, and student conversations from real kindergarten classrooms. These resources can help you interpret experiences from your own classroom as you progress through a unit.

Documentation of Student Growth

You will probably need to develop some sort of system to record and keep track of your observations. A single observation is like a snapshot of a student's experience with a particular activity, but when considered over time, a collection of these snapshots provides an informative and detailed picture of a student. Such observations are useful in documenting and assessing student's growth, as well as in planning curriculum.

Observation Notes A few ideas that teachers have found successful for record keeping are suggested here. The most important consideration is finding a system that really works for you. All too often, keeping observation notes on a class of 20–30 students is overwhelming and time-consuming. Your goal is to find a system that is neither.

Some teachers find that a class list of names is convenient for jotting down their observations. Since the space is limited, it is not possible to write lengthy notes; however, over time, these short observations provide important information.

Other teachers keep a card file or a loose-leaf notebook with a page for each student. When something about a student's thinking strikes them as important, they jot down brief notes and the date.

Some teachers use self-sticking address labels, kept on clipboards around the classroom. After taking notes on individual students, they simply peel off each label and stick it into the appropriate student file or notebook page.

You may find that writing notes at the end of each week works well for you. For some teachers, this process helps them reflect on individual students, on the curriculum, and on the class as a whole. Planning for the next weeks' activities often grows out of these weekly reflections.

Student Portfolios Collecting samples of student work from each unit in a portfolio is another way to document a student's experience that supports your observation notes. In kindergarten, samples of student work may include constructions, patterns, or designs that students have recorded, score sheets from games they have played, and early attempts to record their problem-solving strategies on paper, using pictures, numbers, or words.

The ability to record and represent one's ideas and strategies on paper develops over time. Not all 5- and 6-year-olds will be ready for this. Even when students are ready, what they record will have meaning for them only in the moment—as they work on the activity and make their representation. You can augment this by taking dictation of a student's idea or strategy. This not only helps both you and the student recall the idea, but also gives students a model of how their ideas could be recorded on paper.

Over the school year, student work samples combined with anecdotal observations are valuable resources when you are preparing for family conferences or writing student reports. They help you communicate student growth and progress, both to families and to the students' subsequent teachers.

Assessment Overview

There are two places to turn for a preview of the assessment information in each kindergarten *Investigations* unit. The Assessment Resources column in the Unit Overview chart locates the Observing the Students section for each activity, plus any Teacher Notes and Dialogue Boxes that explain what to look for and what types of responses you might see in your classroom. Additionally, the section called About the Assessment in This Unit gives you a detailed list of questions, keyed to the mathematical emphases for each investigation, to help you observe and assess student growth. This section also includes suggestions for choosing student work to save from the unit.

These examples illustrate record keeping systems used by two different teachers for the kindergarten unit *Collecting, Counting, and Measuring,* one using the class list and the other using individual note cards to record student progress.

> *Emma Ruiz*
>
> 3/19 *Counting Jar: counts 9 balls accurately and makes another set of 9 cubes*
>
> 3/24 *Today's Question: compares data, "13 is 4 more than 9 because the 13 tower is 4 names taller."*
>
> 4/1 *Draws counting Book pictures for 1-6, then adds pgs 7,8,9,10,11 on her own*

Unit: *Collecting, Counting, and Measuring*
Activity: *Inventory Bags*
Date: *10/12 and 10/13*

Alexa • *counting sequence to 50↑* • *counts 1:1 up to 12* • *counts 4 bags accurately*	Luke • *counts to 30, misses 19,20 and 29,30* • *counts by moving objects; 1:1 to 10 objects* • *draws circles for buttons*
Ayesha • *works with Oscar* • *counts to 15 accurately – trouble beyond 15 but Oscar helps* ★ *Meet to check* • *1:1 to 8 objects?* *counting*	Maddy • *difficult to tell how much M. counted herself + how much was done by partner. Work w/ her to see.*
Brendan *absent 10/12, 10/13*	Miyuki • *counts aloud beyond 30 but leaves out 14* • *counts 1:1 up to 10 but doesn't organize objects*
Carlo • *counts objects with difficulty.* • *remove items from bag so he works with 10* • *says numbers to 10, counts objects to 6*	Oscar • *works with Ayesha* • *counts rotely to 20, maybe higher* • *double-checks his count every time – is accurate*
Charlotte • *completed inventory task easily without help* • *counts accurately up to 20 objects* • *represents with numbers*	Ravi • *worked w/ his aide to complete task* • *counts 1:1 to 5 objects* • *difficulty representing quantity w/ pictures*
Felipe • *worked well with Tarik* • *counted ~~_____ bag~~ – 21 in all*	Renata

Mathematical Thinking in Kindergarten

Content of This Unit With this unit, you introduce some of the mathematical materials and processes your kindergarten students will use this year as they explore aspects of number, data, and geometry. Students have a chance to freely explore such mathematical tools as pattern blocks, color tiles, interlocking cubes, and Geoblocks. At the same time, they encounter some important mathematical ideas in four activities that become Classroom Routines.

Two activities—taking daily attendance, and regular use of a Counting Jar—give students repeated practice with counting as they begin to make the connection between number names and the quantities they represent. The calendar is introduced as a tool for keeping track of time; it is also another place to visit the number sequence and to count. Through both the Attendance routine and the activity Today's Question, the class begins to collect and organize data about themselves. While working with the pattern blocks and Geoblocks, students become familiar with a variety of two-dimensional and three-dimensional shapes.

This unit also includes suggestions for organizing and managing the classroom environment as you work to establish a mathematical community.

Connections with Other Units If you are doing the full-year *Investigations* curriculum in the suggested sequence for kindergarten, this is the first of six units. The tools introduced here will be used in subsequent units for activities in counting, pattern-making, sorting, and exploring geometric shapes. The classroom routines introduced in the first unit (Attendance, Counting Jar, Calendar, and Today's Question) are to be continued throughout the year, providing ongoing support for the mathematical work of the other units.

Investigations Curriculum ■ Suggested Kindergarten Sequence

▶ *Mathematical Thinking in Kindergarten* (Introduction)

Pattern Trains and Hopscotch Paths (Exploring Pattern)

Collecting, Counting, and Measuring (Developing Number Sense)

Counting Ourselves and Others (Exploring Data)

Making Shapes and Building Blocks (Exploring Geometry)

How Many in All? (Counting and the Number System)

Investigation 1 ▪ Attendance

Class Sessions	Activities	Pacing
FOCUS TIME (p. 4) Attendance	Our Names and Our Cubes How Many Are We? Making an Attendance Stick Homework: Family Connection	1 session
CHOICE TIME (p. 12)	Exploring Color Tiles Exploring Pattern Blocks Exploring Geoblocks	3–4 sessions

Classroom Routines   Attendance (on a daily basis)

Mathematical Emphasis

- Counting the number of students in the class

- Establishing a one-to-one correspondence between the number of students in the class and a stack of interlocking cubes

- Exploring color tiles and their attributes

- Exploring pattern blocks and their attributes

- Exploring Geoblocks and their attributes

- Using informal language to describe geometric shapes

- Establishing routines for using and caring for manipulative materials

Assessment Resources

Observing the Students:

- Attendance (p. 9)

- Exploring Color Tiles (p. 13)

- Exploring Pattern Blocks (p. 15)

- Exploring Geoblocks (p. 17)

Dialogue Box: I'm Not 8, I'm 5! (p. 11)

Teacher Note: Talking About Pattern Blocks and Geoblocks (p. 22)

Materials

Materials
Interlocking cubes
Dot stickers
Name cards
Clothespins
Color tiles
Pattern blocks
Geoblocks
Scoops
Recording materials (optional): construction paper squares, grid paper, paper pattern blocks, unlined paper, glue sticks, colored pencils, markers, or crayons

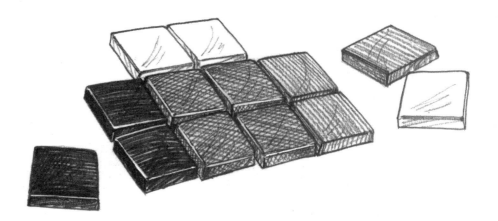

Investigation 2 ▪ Counting Jar

Class Sessions	Activities	Pacing
FOCUS TIME (p. 26) Counting Jar	*Mouse Count* Counting and Showing the Count Counting Out a New Set Sharing How We Counted	1 session
CHOICE TIME (p. 32)	Counting Jar Exploring Color Tiles Exploring Pattern Blocks Exploring Geoblocks	2–3 sessions
Classroom Routines	Attendance (on a daily basis) Counting Jar (weekly or as appropriate)	

Mathematical Emphasis

- Counting a set of objects

- Creating a set of a given size

- Recording numerical information

- Exploring manipulative materials

- Establishing routines for using and caring for manipulative materials

Assessment Resources

Observing the Students:

- Counting Jar (p. 33)

Teacher Note: Counting Is More Than 1, 2, 3 (p. 36)

Teacher Note: Observing Students As They Count (p. 37)

Dialogue Box: You Could Use Dots (p. 39)

Materials

Mouse Count by E. S. Walsh (optional)

Clear container (Counting Jar)

Various countable objects

Index cards

Chart paper

Paper plates

Color tiles

Pattern blocks

Geoblocks

Recording materials (optional)

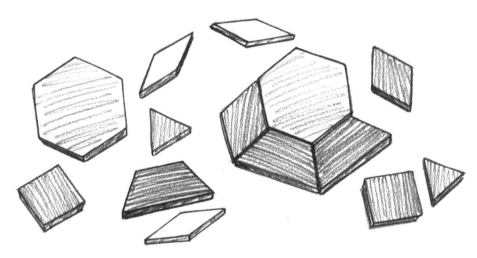

Pattern blocks

Investigation 3 ▪ Calendar

Class Sessions	Activities	Pacing
FOCUS TIME (p. 42) Calendar	*Only Six More Days* Our Calendar	1 session
CHOICE TIME (p. 48)	Exploring Interlocking Cubes Counting Jar Exploring Materials (Teacher's Choice)	3–4 sessions
Classroom Routines	Attendance and Calendar (on a daily basis) Counting Jar (every few days)	

Mathematical Emphasis

- Developing a sense of time (days, weeks)

- Viewing the calendar as a tool for keeping track of time and events

- Counting on the calendar

- Connecting number names, numerals, and quantities

- Exploring interlocking cubes and their attributes

- Establishing routines for using and caring for interlocking cubes and other manipulative materials

Assessment Resources

Observing the Students:

- Calendar (p. 46)

- Exploring Interlocking Cubes (p. 49)

Materials

Only Six More Days by M. Russo (optional)
Classroom calendar
Other sample calendars
Interlocking cubes
Counting Jar
Countable objects
Paper plates
Color tiles
Pattern blocks
Geoblocks
Recording materials (optional)

Interlocking cubes

Investigation 4 ▪ Today's Question

Class Sessions	Activities	Pacing
FOCUS TIME (p. 54) Today's Question	Are You a Girl or a Boy? Looking at Our Data Adding Absent Students	1 session
CHOICE TIME (p. 59)	Counting Jar Exploring Materials (Teacher's Choice)	2–3 sessions
Classroom Routines	Attendance and Calendar (on a daily basis) Counting Jar (every few days)	

Mathematical Emphasis

- Collecting data that fall into two groups

- Counting and comparing the number of students in different groups

- Establishing one-to-one correspondence between a group and the data collected

Assessment Resources

Observing the Students:

- Today's Question (p. 57)

Dialogue Box: What Do You Notice? (p. 60)

Materials

Name cards or name pins

Attendance stick (cubes)

Chart paper

Counting Jar

Countable objects

Paper plates

Interlocking cubes

Color tiles

Pattern blocks

Geoblocks

Recording materials (optional)

Geoblocks

Following are the basic materials needed for the activities in this unit. Many items can be purchased from the publisher, either individually or in the Teacher Resource Package and the Student Materials Kit for kindergarten. Detailed information is available on the *Investigations* order form. To obtain this form, call toll-free 1-800-872-1100 and ask for a Dale Seymour customer service representative.

Snap™ Cubes (interlocking cubes): class set, or 1 tub of 100 per 4–6 students

Color tiles: 2 buckets of 400 per class

Pattern blocks: 1 bucket per 4–6 students

Geoblocks: 2 sets per class

Teddy bear counters: 1 set per 4–6 students

Collections of countable materials, such as Styrofoam peanuts, pencils, erasers, markers, lids, buttons, blocks, keys, shells

Spring-clip clothespins: 1 per student

Paper pattern blocks: 2–3 sets (optional)

Clear plastic container to use as a Counting Jar

Paper plates: 1 per student

Classroom calendar, with pockets or removable numbers

Mouse Count by Ellen Stoll Walsh (optional)

Only Six More Days by Marisabina Russo (optional)

Chart paper

Card stock or tagboard: 2–3 sheets

Index cards or paper cut into rectangles 4 by 6 inches

Student photos (optional)

Colored construction paper (optional)

Unlined paper and coloring materials (colored pencils, markers, crayons)

Dot stickers

Tape

Glue sticks (optional)

The following materials are provided at the end of this unit as blackline masters.

Family Letter (p. 80)

Teaching Resources:

    Pattern Block Cutouts (p. 81)

    One-Inch Grid Paper (p. 87)

    Choice Board Art (p. 88)

Related Children's Literature

Numbers and Counting

Crews, Donald. *Ten Black Dots*. New York: Greenwillow Books, 1986.

Feelings, Muriel. *Moja Means One: Swahili Counting Book*. First Pied Piper Printing, 1976.

Garne, S. T. *One White Sail: A Caribbean Counting Book*. New York: Green Tiger Press/Simon and Schuster, 1992.

Grossman, Virginia. *Ten Little Rabbits*. San Francisco, CA: Chronicle Books, 1991.

Hoban, Tana. *Count and See*. New York: Macmillan, 1972.

Onyefulu, Ifeoma. *Emeka's Gift: An African Counting Story*. New York: Cobblehill Books/Dutton, 1995.

Walsh, Ellen Stoll. *Mouse Count*. New York: Harcourt Brace Jovanovich, 1991.

Calendar and Time

Russo, Marisabina. *Only Six More Days*. New York: Puffin Books, 1992.

Mathematical Thinking in Kindergarten is an introduction to the mathematical content, materials, processes, and ways of working that students will use throughout the year in the *Investigations* curriculum. Through the work in this unit, students

- explore the materials they will be using to model mathematical situations
- talk about how to solve mathematical problems
- work with peers as they share ideas and materials
- rely on their own thinking, and learn from the thinking of others

With these investigations, you introduce four of the routines that become regular and familiar activities over the kindergarten year. Students also have many chances to freely explore the materials— color tiles, pattern blocks, Geoblocks, interlocking cubes—they will be using for mathematical work in the coming months and years. This work involves the class in the three areas of the *Investigations* curriculum: number, data, and space (geometry).

Number concepts are part of all four routines, as students practice counting in a variety of situations—counting themselves in class, counting a few small items in a jar, counting days on the calendar, and counting names on a chart. Over time, students begin to learn the counting sequence, to connect number names with quantities, to establish one-to-one correspondence, and to find ways to record numerical information. They also have the chance to compare quantities and begin to use the terms *more, less,* and *same.*

Work with data analysis is part of the Attendance routine as well as Today's Question, as students collect, count, represent, and interpret data about themselves. While determining how many are *here* or *not here,* or how many are *girls* and how many are *boys,* students are counting and comparing quantities that have real meaning to them. As they analyze the two groups, they explore part-whole relationships. Again they consider, Which is more? Which is less? How many more or less?

Pattern blocks and Geoblocks offer kindergartners an introduction to geometry. Students explore the ways that these two- and three-dimensional shapes fit together and notice their special attributes. Through this exploration, they intuitively learn much about the characteristics of both sets of blocks in preparation for later experiences in classifying, describing, and defining shapes.

For most kindergarten students, this may be their first experience with solving mathematical problems and trying to explain their thinking to others. It also may be their first experience with using things like blocks and colored cubes in structured activities instead of free play. Even the process of taking out specific materials and putting them away may be unfamiliar to some. This unit is a time to focus on the development of these processes; to spend time establishing routines and expectations; to communicate to students your own interest in and respect for their mathematical ideas; to assure students that you want to know about their *thinking,* not just their answers; and to support students as they work on problems in ways that make sense to them. As the unit unfolds, a mathematical community begins to take shape—a community that you and your students are together responsible for creating and maintaining.

At the beginning of each investigation, the Mathematical Emphasis section tells you what is most important for students to learn about during that investigation. Many of these mathematical understandings and processes are difficult and complex. Students gradually learn more and more about each idea over many years of schooling. Individual students will begin and end the unit with different levels of knowledge and skill, but all will become familiar with ways of thinking mathematically about introductory concepts in number, data, and geometry.

Throughout the *Investigations* curriculum, there are many opportunities for ongoing daily assessment as you observe, listen to, and interact with students at work. You can use almost any activity in this unit to assess your students' needs and strengths. Listed below are questions to help you focus your observations in each investigation. You may want to keep track of your observations for each student to help you plan your curriculum and monitor students' growth. Suggestions for documenting student growth can be found in the section About Assessment (p. I-8).

The primary purpose of this unit is to introduce ongoing routines in mathematics. Because you will be doing these routines all year, the activities in these investigations are useful for assessing students' development over time.

Investigation 1: Attendance

■ How familiar are students with the process of counting? Do they say one number name for each person they count? How comfortably (and high) can they count orally? Do students know the sequence of number names? Do they forget any of the number names? Which ones? Do they skip certain numbers or mix the order of the names? Which ones? Do they self-correct? Do they hear mistakes in the counting sequence if someone else makes them?

■ Do students relate the total number of students in class to the total number of cubes in the Attendance Stick in any way?

■ How do students explore the pattern blocks? the color tiles? the Geoblocks? Do they lay them flat, using them to cover a space or area? Do they stand them on edge or build vertically with them? Do they stack them? Do they use them to engage in dramatic play?

■ How do they describe the materials? Do they refer to them by shape? by color? by size?

■ Do students have a sense that pairs or combinations of pattern blocks and Geoblocks can be substituted for other blocks?

Investigation 2: Counting Jar

■ Are students able to accurately count a set of objects? Do they know the sequence of number names? Do they forget or mix the order of some of the numbers? Which ones?

■ Do students have a system for counting the objects in the jar? Do they remove one object at a time? Do they dump out the contents and randomly count? Do they organize them in some way? Do students put each object back in the jar as they count it? Do they double-check their count?

■ How do students record the number of objects they think are in the jar? Do they use pictures to represent the objects? Do they use numbers? Do they have a strategy for figuring out how to write a particular number? Do they just know how some numbers look? Do they refer to the number line or calendar or other examples of written numerals?

■ Are students able to create a new, equivalent set of objects?

■ How do students explore and talk about the manipulative materials available during Choice Time? How do their activities with these materials change and develop over time?

Investigation 3: Calendar

■ What do students know about calendars? What do they notice about the classroom calendar? What information do they attend to (the letters, numerals, tags for special days, colors)?

■ How comfortable are students counting on the calendar? Do students know the sequence of number names? Do they forget or mix the order of some of the numbers? Which ones?

■ How do students explore the materials that continue to be available? How does their exploration of these materials change and develop over time?

■ How do student explore the interlocking cubes? the Geoblocks? What kinds of constructions or shapes do they make? How do they describe the materials and their creations?

Investigation 4: Today's Question

- Do students seem to understand what the data represents? Can they describe in their own words what information is being collected?

- What features of the representation do students notice? Do they comment on relevant features of the representation and the data? (For example, "There are more boys than girls," or "There are 12 girls on the graph.")

- Are students able to make comparisons between the two groups? If the two groups are not equal, can they figure out which group has more? How do they do this? Do they compare the number of responses in each group?

- Do students recognize that there is a one-to-one correspondence between the number of responses on the graph and the number of students in the class?

Thinking and Working in Mathematics

This unit provides the chance for you to observe students' work habits and communication skills. Think about these questions as you decide which routines, processes, and materials will require the most support.

- How comfortable are students in various types of work situations? Are they able to work alone? with a partner? Do they participate in whole-group discussions?

- How do students respond to Choice Time? Are they self-directed and able to make choices independently? Do students move comfortably between activities, or do they stick with a familiar and safe choice? Do students get involved in each activity, or do they move around quickly from one activity to another?

- How do students interact with peers? Do they share ideas? share materials? work cooperatively? Or do they prefer to work independently? How do they handle and resolve disagreements?

- Can students express their ideas orally? Who participates in discussions?

- Do students have ideas about how they might record their work, either with words, numbers, or pictures?

- What types of materials or activities do individual students seem most (or least) comfortable with?

- How do students explore materials? Do they initiate their own ideas, observe others, or follow given prompts or suggestions? Can they follow an idea through to completion, or do they begin one construction and then quickly abandon it for another and then another?

In the *Investigations* curriculum, mathematical vocabulary is introduced naturally during the activities. We don't ask students to learn definitions of new terms; rather, they come to understand such words as *triangle, add, compare, data,* and *graph* by hearing them used frequently in discussion as they investigate new concepts. This approach is compatible with current theories of second-language acquisition, which emphasize the use of new vocabulary in meaningful contexts while students are actively involved with objects, pictures, and physical movement.

Listed below are some key words used in this unit that will not be new to most English speakers at this age level, but may be unfamiliar to students with limited English proficiency. You will want to spend additional time working on these words with your students who are learning English. If your students are working with a second-language teacher, you might enlist your colleague's aid in familiarizing students with these words, before and during this unit. In the classroom, look for opportunities for students to hear and use these words. Activities you can use to present the words are given in the appendix, Vocabulary Support for Second-Language Learners (p. 78).

name Students use their names in two routines, Attendance (Investigation 1) and Today's Question (Investigation 4).

how many? This basic phrase recurs in every investigation, as students are learning to count themselves, small objects, days on a calendar, and names on a list to determine *how many.*

big, little, tiny, same, different Words that describe size and likeness are likely to come up as students share their ideas about the materials they are exploring, especially pattern blocks and Geoblocks.

colors: red, yellow, blue, tan, orange, green, purple, black, white, brown Also likely to come up frequently in discussion are the six colors of the pattern blocks, which overlap with the ten colors of the interlocking cubes, the four colors of the color tiles, and the colors of other common primary materials, such as teddy bear counters.

Multicultural Extensions for All Students

Whenever possible, encourage students to share words, objects, customs, or any aspects of daily life from their own cultures and backgrounds that are relevant to the activities in this unit. For example, in the Calendar routine (Investigation 3), make a point of highlighting special days or events that are important to the cultures represented in your classroom. Also note that a number of counting books with themes related to other cultures are included in the list of Related Children's Literature (p. I-15).

This curriculum is a guide, not a prescription or recipe. We tested these activities in many different classrooms, representing a range of students and teachers, and we revised our ideas constantly as we learned from students and teachers alike. Every time we tried a curriculum unit in a classroom, no matter how many times it had been tried and revised before, we discovered new ideas we wanted to add and changes we wanted to make. This process could be endless, but at some point we have to decide that the curriculum works well enough with a wide range of students.

We cannot anticipate the needs and strengths of your particular students this particular year. We believe that the only way for good curriculum to be used well is for teachers to participate in continually modifying it. Your role is to observe and listen carefully to your students, to try to understand how they are thinking, and to make decisions, based on your observations, about what they need next. Modifications to the curriculum that you will need to consider throughout the year include:

- changing the quantities being explored to make the problem more accessible or more challenging for particular students

- repeating activities with which students need more experience

- engaging students in extensions and further questions

- rearranging pairs or small groups so that students learn from a variety of their peers

Your students can help you set the right level of pace and challenge. We have found that, when given choices of activities, students often do choose the right level of difficulty for themselves. You can encourage students to do this by urging them to find problems that are "not too easy, not too hard, but just right." Help students understand that doing mathematics does *not* mean knowing the answer right away. Tell students often, "A good problem for you is a problem that makes you think hard and work hard. You might have to try more than one way of doing it before you figure it out."

The *Investigations* curriculum provides more than enough material for any student. Variations and extensions to the activities offer a variety of additional options for exploring the big mathematical ideas of each unit. Many teachers also have favorite activities that they integrate into this curriculum. We encourage you to be an active partner with us in creating the way this curriculum can work best for your students.

Investigations

INVESTIGATION 1

Attendance

Focus Time

Attendance (p. 4)

During whole-group meeting, students use name cards or "name pins" and interlocking cubes to collect classroom attendance information. They establish the number of students in their class by counting the group in two different ways, then construct an attendance stick of interlocking cubes, one for each student. This activity is suggested as an ongoing daily classroom routine for the kindergarten *Investigations* curriculum.

Choice Time

Exploring Color Tiles (p. 12)

In the Choice Time format, students work independently on several activities, often as a follow-up to the concepts introduced in Focus Time. For this introductory unit, Choice Time is devoted primarily to exploration of the materials students will be using throughout the year in mathematics. They start by exploring the color tiles, a set of one-inch square tiles in four colors, useful for pattern, counting, sorting, and number-related activities.

Exploring Pattern Blocks (p. 14)

Students explore pattern blocks, a set of six flat blocks recognizable by their two-dimensional shapes, useful for pattern, counting, sorting, and geometry activities.

Exploring Geoblocks (p. 16)

Students engage in free play with the Geoblocks, a set of three-dimensional wooden blocks useful for pattern, counting, sorting, and geometry activities.

Mathematical Emphasis

- Collecting information through counting
- One-to-one correspondence
- Beginning to connect numerals and number names to the quantities they represent
- Exploring materials that will be used in this unit and throughout the curriculum
- Establishing classroom routines that will continue throughout the year

Teacher Support

Teacher Notes

About Choice Time (p. 18)

Supporting Students' Free Play (p. 21)

Talking About Pattern Blocks and Geoblocks (p. 22)

Dialogue Boxes

I'm Not 8, I'm 5! (p. 11)

Flowers, Dancers, and Pattern Block Walls (p. 23)

Name cards

What to Plan Ahead of Time

Focus Time Materials

Attendance

- Interlocking cubes of only one color: 1 per student
- Dot stickers (small enough to fit on the side of an interlocking cube): 1 per student
- Name cards: 1 per student. Print each student's name on a card about 2 by 3 inches. If possible, include a small photo.
- Name pins: 1 per student, as an optional alternative to name cards. Print each student's name on both sides of a clothespin so that the name is right side up whether the clip is to the right or to the left.
- Display board for name pins: a sturdy board, about 8 inches wide and 36 inches tall, divided vertically into Here and Not Here columns.

Choice Time Materials

Exploring Color Tiles

- Color tiles: 1 bucket per 8–10 students
- Small cups to use as scoops
- Trays or sturdy cardboard mats (optional)
- One-inch grid paper: 1 pad, or duplicate from master on p. 87 (optional)
- One-inch paper squares cut from construction paper in colors to match the tiles (optional)
- Glue sticks (optional)
- Unlined paper and coloring materials, available

Exploring Pattern Blocks

- Pattern blocks: 1 bucket per 4–6 students
- Small cups to use as scoops
- Paper pattern blocks: 1 manufactured set, or prepare from masters on pp. 81–86 (optional)
- Unlined paper and coloring materials, available

Exploring Geoblocks

- Geoblocks: 2 sets per classroom, divided into smaller sets (see p. 63)
- Other classroom sets of building blocks (optional)
- Unlined paper and drawing materials, available

Family Connection

- Family letter: 1 per family

Focus Time

Attendance

What Happens

Students are introduced to a routine for taking and thinking about daily attendance. As a whole group, they count the number of students in their class. Each student contributes one interlocking cube to make an attendance stick, representing *how many* students are in the class. A display of name cards or name pins provides information about *who* these people are. Students' work focuses on:

■ counting the number of students in the class

■ establishing one-to-one correspondence between the number of students in the class and a stack of interlocking cubes

Materials and Preparation

■ Provide name cards, about 2 by 3 inches, each printed with a student's first name. Add a school photo or snapshot of the child if possible. You may display these cards on the floor or on a display board. For use with a display board, attach a suitable fastener (such as a small piece of Velcro or magnetic tape) to the back of each card. Name cards should be durable; they are suggested for use again in Investigation 4 and may also be useful for other activities.

■ As an alternative to name cards, make name pins by printing each student's name on both sides of a wooden spring-clip clothespin. Have available a tall board divided into Here and Not Here sections (see illustration, p. 67).

■ Spread out the prepared name cards (or name pins) on a surface where everyone can see and reach them. Place an interlocking cube on top of each card or beside each pin. All cubes should be the same color.

■ Number a sheet of dot stickers from 1 through the total number in your class, writing one number on each sticker.

Our Names and Our Cubes

Note: Attendance is one of the suggested classroom routines for the kindergarten *Investigations* curriculum. Classroom routines are familiar activities that occur in many kindergarten classrooms throughout the year. Many of them offer opportunities to explore rich mathematics in a meaningful context. For more information about the Attendance routine, including variations and extensions to use throughout the year, see About Classroom Routines: Attendance (p. 65).

Introduce this activity to the whole class during a group meeting. If space allows, plan to have students sit in a circle or semicircle so they can see you and each other.

For this first attendance activity, students will need to find their name card or name pin on the table, take the cube they find with it, and bring only the cube with them to meeting, leaving the name cards or pins on the table. Plan to help those students who have difficulty locating their names.

After all students have picked up their cubes, gather up any remaining name cards or pins and cubes (for absent students) and bring them with you to the group meeting area. Keep them in view. In addition to these items, you will need the sheet of numbered dot stickers you have prepared.

How Many Are We?

If you are introducing this activity early in the school year, help students acknowledge their classmates. You may want to go around the circle for introductions, with each student saying his or her name. Or you might welcome each student individually and introduce him or her to the group.

Remind students that as they gathered in the meeting area, each of them found their name on the table and took the cube that was with their name. Display on the floor the names and cubes of any students who are not present.

Look carefully around you. These are the people who are going to be in our class this year. Every day when we come to school, we will see if everyone is here. On some days, some of you might not come to school because you are sick. Every day, we will need to figure out who is here and who is not here.

Draw attention to the name cards (or pins) for the absent students. Point out that even though those students are not here today, they too will be part of the class this year. Next turn students' attention to *how many* of them are in the class.

Another thing we will need to figure out each day is how many of you are here in class, and how many of you are not here. Look around the circle. How could we figure out how many children are here in our class today? Who has an idea?

Students may have a variety of ideas for finding the number in the class. Commonly they suggest that one student go around and count each person, or that the teacher count everyone.

If this is the first time you have counted the number of students in the class as a group, you may want to model the process by going around the circle and saying one number as you point to each person. At the beginning of kindergarten, you may have many students who are unfamiliar with the sequence of numbers and with counting as a process. Some students will have had little experience with counting or hearing others count. Others will have counted before, but may have trouble with the counting sequence past 5.

I'm going to go around the circle and point to each person as I count all of you. See if you can help me as I count the number of people in our class.

Encourage students to count together with you. Counting in unison will often carry the class as a whole much farther in the counting sequence than many individuals in the class could actually count by themselves. Most likely, one or two children will be able to count to the total number of students in the class, but do not be surprised or concerned if you are the only one saying the last few numbers. Students learn the counting sequence and how to count by having many opportunities to count and to see and hear others count. The **Teacher Note**, Counting Is More Than 1, 2, 3 (p. 36), offers more information on how kindergarten students learn to count.

We counted each person in the circle and found out that there are 24 students here today. But we know from picking up our cubes that Tiana is not here today, because her cube was left on the table with her name card. So, when everyone is here, there will be 25 children in our class.

Counting Around the Circle After you have counted the number of students present, introduce the class to counting around the circle, or counting off, as another way to count and double-check the number of students that are present.

Sometimes it's a good idea to count things more than one time. This is called double-checking. We can double-check the number of people who are here today by *counting around* our circle. Here's the way counting around the circle works: The first person to count will say "1," and the second person will say "2." What do you think the third person will say? What about the fourth person?

Designate one student in the circle as the first person and begin counting around the group. When first introducing this method of counting, you can help by pointing to individual students when it is their turn to say a number. Some students will probably need help knowing what number comes next in the counting sequence. Encourage the group to help one another figure out the next number. This helps establish a climate in which students are comfortable asking for and giving help to others.

It takes time for students to understand the activity of counting around the circle, both the procedure itself and what it means. For some students, it will not be apparent that the number they say when you point to them stands for the number of people that have counted thus far. When they are first learning to "count off," kindergartners commonly relate the number that they say to a more familiar number, their age. Expect to hear, for example, "But I'm not 8, I'm 5." When this happens, be prepared to explain that the purpose of counting off is to find out how many students are in the circle and that the number 8 stands for all of the people who have been counted so far. See the **Dialogue Box**, I'm Not 8, I'm 5! (p. 11), for the way this conversation unfolded in one class.

Activity

Making an Attendance Stick

Ask students to show you the cubes they picked up when they entered the meeting area. Before collecting and counting the cubes, make sure every student has one. Keep the name cards or pins and the cubes of any absent students close by; you will add their cubes to the end of the attendance stick.

We just figured out that we have 24 children in our classroom today. When you joined the group this morning, everyone took one cube. Suppose we collected all the cubes and snapped them together. How many cubes do you think we would have?

Some students will recognize that the number of cubes should be the same as the total number of students in the class, while many other kindergartners will not see the connection between the two. As students offer their ideas, encourage them to explain their thinking. Although this can be a challenging task for many young students, encouraging them to try sets the tone for talking about mathematics and explaining answers. See the **Teacher Note**, Encouraging Students to Think, Reason, and Share Ideas (p. 50), for more information on this.

When students have shared their ideas, collect the cubes one by one and snap them together into a tower. As you add each cube to the tower, encourage students to count with you, saying one number for each cube.

We made a cube tower. It has 24 cubes in it because there are 24 students in our class today.

In order to assemble an attendance stick that represents the total number in your class when everyone is present, you will need to add cubes for those who are absent. Once again, direct attention to the names and cubes of absent students.

When you came into our group meeting today, you each took a cube that you found with your name. Since Tiana is not here today, she did not take a cube. But she will be in our class, so we need to add her cube to our tower. Right now our tower has 24 cubes in it because there are 24 children in class today. When we add Tiana's cube, how many cubes will be in our tower?

As you add a cube for each absent child, some students may be able to tell you the new number of cubes in the tower. However, for many kindergarten students, numbers in the 20's seem very large and may be unfamiliar. One goal of this classroom routine is not just to familiarize students with the counting sequence of numbers above 10, but also to help them relate these numbers to the quantities that they represent. While the total number of students in your class is likely to be a large number, it still holds a great deal of meaning for students because it represents *them*.

When you have added cubes for absent students, verify the total number in the tower by counting the cubes together with the class.

This is a very special tower of cubes that we call an attendance stick. It has one cube for each child in our class when *everyone* is here. Every day, we will use our attendance stick when we talk about the number of people who are here and the number of people who are not here.

If you have time and the students remain attentive, use the dot stickers that you have prepared and label the cubes with numbers, in order, while students watch. If you do not have time during this session, plan to label the attendance stick with the numbered dots the next time you take attendance.

Observing the Students

During the Attendance routine, watch for the following:

- What ideas do students have for figuring out the total number of children in the classroom?

- How familiar are students with the process of counting? Do they say one number name for each person they count? How comfortably (and high) can they count orally? Do students know the sequence of number names? Do they forget any of the number names? Which ones? Do they skip certain numbers or mix the order of the names? Which ones? Do they self-correct? Do they hear mistakes in the counting sequence if someone else makes them?

- Do students relate the total number of students in class to the total number of cubes in the attendance stick? Do they know that the two amounts should be the same?

Note: Although the name cards or name pins have not been used extensively during these introductory activities, you can use them on subsequent days to vary and add interest to the Attendance routine. Name cards or pins displayed in Here and Not Here groupings give a clear picture of the day's attendance and offer more opportunities for counting. See the section About Classroom Routines: Attendance (p. 65) for more information.

Focus Time Follow-Up

 **Homework**

Family Connection Send home the signed family letter or *Investigations* at Home to introduce the work you will be doing in this first unit of the *Investigations* curriculum.

Choice Time

Setting Up Choices Choice Time is a classroom structure suggested throughout the kindergarten *Investigations* curriculum. It is an opportunity for students to engage in a variety of activities centered around similar mathematical ideas and content.

Many kindergarten teachers organize their classroom environment so that small groups of students work at centers or stations on a variety of activities. If you already do this, find ways of incorporating these Choice Time activities into the structure that works for your classroom. The two most important aspects are giving students many opportunities to return to the same activities, and encouraging them to participate in the decisions about what they are going to do. See the **Teacher Note**, About Choice Time (p. 18), for more information on scheduling, managing, and helping students work within this special structure.

Three Choices Since this unit is introductory in nature, Choice Time is used to introduce many of the manipulative materials students will be using in activities throughout the year. You will be establishing routines and procedures for using materials, as well as helping students learn to work with classmates and use their class time in productive and engaging ways. The following three activities are suggested for the first Choice Time. See the **Teacher Note**, From the Classroom: Getting Started (p. 34), for advice from one teacher who struggled with the first Choice Time of the school year.

Exploring Color Tiles

Exploring Pattern Blocks

Exploring Geoblocks

I'm Not 8, I'm 5!

During attendance, this class found that there are 24 students present. Now they double-check the total number by counting around the circle. When a student is puzzled that his number is different from his age, the teacher helps students make sense out of what is being counted and what the numbers mean.

We found out there are 24 children in school today. When we count things, it's a good idea to count again as a way of double-checking. One way to double-check the number of people is by counting off. Here's how it works: The first person will say "one," and the next person will say "two."

Henry: And the next person will say "three."

Yes, the next person will say "three," and that will tell us that three people have counted so far. Let's try this. Renata, you start and be the first one to say a number.

Renata: One!

Brendan: Two!

Justine: Three!

So how many people have counted so far? How can we tell?

Renata: One, two, three *[points to herself and her two neighbors].* You just count them.

So far, then, we have three people who have counted. Tarik, you're next.

Tarik: Four!

Thomas: Five!

And now how many people have counted? *[A few students call out "Five."]*

Luke: I'm 5, too! *[He holds up five fingers.]*

Yes, you are 5 years old, aren't you? Lots of people are 5 in our class. Sometimes numbers tell us how many years old people are, and sometimes they tell us *how many* of us there are. When Thomas said 5, it was because five people have counted so far. Let's count them.

The students count from 1 to 5 as the teacher points to the first five in the circle. The next few students continue the count.

Ayesha: Six.

Xing-Qi: Seven.

Maddy: Eight. But I'm not 8, I'm 5.

Yes, you are 5 years old, too. Just like Luke, who said he is 5 years old. In fact, how many people are 5 years old? *[About three-fourths of the students raise their hands.]* **Lots of people are 5 years old in our class. Later we can figure out how many. Who can explain to Maddy why she said the number 8?**

Renata: It's because you are 8 people. See, I'm one, but I'm really 5, too. *[She gets up to count each person in the circle.]* He's two, and she's three, four, five, six, seven, and you're eight.

At this point the teacher decides to have Renata continue to point to students as they say their number. Renata is a confident counter and seems to understand the meaning of counting around the circle. Near the end, when some students are unable to say the next number in the sequence, Renata says it for them.

Oscar: 23.

Charlotte: 24.

Renata: There are 24 people here.

Counting around the circle was a challenging task for these kindergartners. Remember that this was the first time they'd done the activity, and it was also the beginning of the school year. Students become familiar with the mechanics of this routine as it is repeated over time. As they have more experiences with counting groups of people or objects, students begin to make sense out of counting and what the numbers in the counting sequence mean.

Exploring Color Tiles

What Happens

Students explore color tiles, a set of one-inch square tiles in four colors, useful for pattern, counting, sorting, and number-related activities. Their work focuses on:

- exploring color tiles and their attributes
- establishing routines for using and caring for color tiles

Materials and Preparation

- Set out containers of color tiles, 1 bucket per 8–10 students. You might also include a small cup or container to use as a scoop (optional).
- If you have trays or sturdy cardboard mats, students might use these to save or share their designs and constructions.

Activity

Briefly introduce color tiles to the class, explaining where they can be found and how they will be used and cared for. For more information on this material, see the **Teacher Note**, About Color Tiles (p. 61).

With the introduction of any new material, it is important to establish clear ground rules. The **Teacher Note**, Materials as Tools for Learning (p. 38), offers tips on establishing routines for using and caring for manipulatives you'll be using all year.

If you plan to have students save or share their color tile constructions and designs, you might make available trays or sturdy cardboard mats. Designs built on these can be moved more easily and quickly.

As Choice Time begins, reassure students about the availability of these materials in the classroom over time. While not everyone can work with the same materials at once, they will take turns and everyone will have lots of chances to visit each station.

Students need many opportunities to use a material in order to become familiar with its characteristics and what can be done with it. They need time to freely explore any material and use it however they like before they can be expected to use it in a more focused or specific activity. The remaining units in the *Investigations* kindergarten sequence assume that students have had numerous opportunities to explore the manipulative materials introduced in this first unit.

As you observe during Choice Time, gather information about how students make choices and involve themselves with activities.

■ Do students stick with the same material for a period of time, or do they move quickly from activity to activity?

■ Do students work alone or in pairs? Are they able to share materials, space and ideas? Are they interested the work of others?

As students work specifically with color tiles, consider the following:

■ What do students create with the tiles? Do they lay the blocks flat to make designs or pictures? Do they stand them on edge or build vertically with them? Do they stack them?

■ Do they use the tiles to make repeating patterns (red, blue, red, blue)?

■ How do students describe the tiles and their creations? Do they refer to them by shape? by color?

If some students seem to need guidance, you might pose a particular task, as discussed in the **Teacher Note**, Supporting Students' Free Play (p. 21). However, at this point, it is more fruitful for students to explore the materials in their own ways, without a particular task to do.

Sharing Ideas Plan a few brief group discussions when students can share the work they have been doing with color tiles. If you have noted some students who are using the tiles in interesting ways—for example, to make color patterns—you might ask them to share their work.

Some students quickly discover that the tiles can be set up in domino-like snakes and toppled over in sequence. Rather than prohibit this sort of play, we suggest allowing students to use the tiles in whatever way they choose, while keeping within the limits of responsible play and activity. This way, when you later ask them to use the tiles for a specific task, they may be less tempted to play around with them. Some teachers even set up a special table for building these domino sequences. When the builders are ready, the entire class gathers for the topple-over. In these classrooms, the novelty and excitement soon disperses and students move on to using the tiles in other ways.

Variation

Once students have had a chance to explore the tiles, some may be interested in recording their designs or patterns. This can be done either by gluing down paper squares of the same color or by coloring the design on one-inch grid paper.

Exploring Pattern Blocks

What Happens

Students explore pattern blocks, a material they will use all year for work with patterns, counting, sorting, and geometry. Their work focuses on:

■ exploring pattern blocks and their attributes

■ using informal language to describe geometric shapes

■ establishing routines for using and caring for pattern blocks

Materials and Preparation

■ Make available your class set of pattern blocks, allowing 1 bin per 4–6 students. Also provide small containers to use as scoops (optional).

■ Familiarize yourself with these shapes and their relationships to one another. Also read the **Teacher Notes**, About Pattern Blocks (p. 62) and Talking About Pattern Blocks and Geoblocks (p. 22).

Activity

Briefly introduce the pattern blocks to the whole group. As with the color tiles, you will want to discuss where the materials are stored and how they will be used and cared for.

Ask if students are familiar with the blocks, how they have used them in the past, and if they know the names of any of them. While some kindergarten students may know the correct geometric terms, many will not. The **Dialogue Box**, Flowers, Dancers, and Pattern Block Walls (p. 23), demonstrates how kindergartners typically describe pattern block shapes. See the **Teacher Note**, Talking About Pattern Blocks and Geoblocks (p. 22), for ways you can introduce the mathematical vocabulary while you talk about the shapes with your students.

Set up the pattern blocks as one of several stations or centers for free exploration. You could use tables, clusters of desks, or floor space as work places. Explain that each center can accommodate a specific number of students. Depending on how you've organized your classroom, this could be indicated by the number of chairs at a certain table or by posting the information on a Choice Board.

- How do students use the pattern blocks? Do they lay the blocks flat to make designs or pictures? Do they stand them on edge or build vertically with them? Do they stack them?

- How do they describe the different pattern blocks? Do they refer to them by shape? by color?

- Do they have a sense that pairs or combinations of blocks can be substituted for other blocks? For example, do they substitute two trapezoids for a hexagon, or two triangles for a blue rhombus?

See the **Teacher Note**, Supporting Students' Free Play (p. 21), and the **Dialogue Box**, Flowers, Dancers and Pattern Block Walls (p. 23), for ideas about helping students structure and focus their explorations and for particular problems you can set for students.

Sharing Ideas While pattern blocks are an available choice, periodically encourage students to talk about the materials in an open discussion.

Who can tell us something you noticed about the pattern blocks? Who noticed something different?

Even if this discussion is very brief, it will give you some ideas about how students describe shapes.

Some students may be interested in sharing the designs and constructions they are making with the pattern blocks. Since students' work will not be very portable, you may want to set aside time to have students walk around and look at work in progress. Or, have students build their designs on sturdy cardboard or a tray for transport to group meeting. Discussion can then focus on different ways students have used the blocks. Offering students opportunities to share their work and see that of others stimulates new ideas and thinking among even the youngest of students.

Also hold brief group discussions about any issues that come up as students work with the materials. For example, if there are problems with sharing, students could role-play a situation that has come up in the classroom, and then talk about what works and what doesn't work.

Variation

Some students may be interested in recording their work, which can be done by gluing paper pattern block shapes onto paper or tagboard. Manufactured shapes are available, or you can make your own with the blackline masters on pages 81–86. Copy these shapes onto colored paper and cut apart. Store in separate plastic bags.

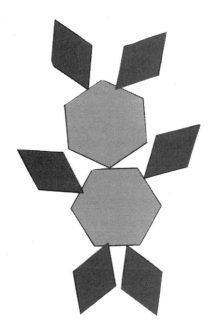

Exploring Geoblocks

What Happens

Students explore Geoblocks, a set of three-dimensional wooden blocks useful for pattern, counting, sorting, and geometry activities. Their work focuses on:

■ exploring Geoblocks and their attributes

■ using informal language to describe geometric shapes

■ establishing routines for using and caring for Geoblocks

Materials and Preparation

■ Provide 1 or 2 sets of Geoblocks, separated into smaller sets. See the **Teacher Note**, About Geoblocks (p. 63), for ideas on how to sort the blocks and for more information about the shapes included in each set.

Activity

While some students may be familiar with other wooden building blocks, they are unlikely to have had previous experience with Geoblocks. Gather students together in a circle and display a set of these blocks.

These are a special type of block, called Geoblocks. Geoblocks are another tool we use to explore mathematics. Look carefully at the blocks. What are some things you notice about them?

Until students have had opportunities to work closely with the blocks, they may remark only on obvious attributes such as color, material, and possibly shape, especially by relating them to the shapes of familiar objects in the real world. They are likely to name things they could build with the blocks.

Explain where and how the Geoblocks can be used and cared for, as discussed in the **Teacher Note**, Materials as Tools for Learning (p. 38).

During Choice Time, the Geoblocks will be one of the materials that you might use. There are only [2 sets] of Geoblocks, so you will have to take turns. If you don't get a chance to build with these blocks today, please don't worry. These blocks, like pattern blocks and color tiles, will be a part of Choice Time for a long time.

Though students may not fully understand the continuing availability of these materials until they experience the patterns and rhythms of the classroom over time, you can keep reminding them, to reassure those who are concerned about not getting a turn.

Observing the Students

Gather information about how your students work with the materials and what ideas about geometric shapes they bring to their work.

- How do students use the Geoblocks? What sorts of constructions do they make? Do they build primarily vertically? Do they stack blocks? Do they build more horizontally, covering space? Do they use them for dramatic play? For example, a group of students in one class called the tiny cubes "gold," which they stored in a treasure box made of prisms.

- How do they describe the different Geoblocks? Do they describe differences in size? Do they notice that some of the faces (they will probably call them "sides") are squares, some are rectangles, and some are triangles? What words do they use to talk about these shapes?

- Do students have a sense that pairs or combinations of blocks can be substituted for other blocks? For example, do they put two (or more) Geoblocks together to match another Geoblock?

Some students will look hard for a particular block, perhaps a duplicate of one they already have. The way the set is designed, several blocks have only a few copies. When students are having trouble finding a particular block, encourage them to think about other possible ways to make a block that is the same size and shape. This can also be a helpful solution for resolving difficulties with sharing.

Sharing Ideas While Geoblocks are an available choice, periodically ask students to talk about what they have noticed about the materials.

What sorts of things have you been doing with the Geoblocks? How are the Geoblocks the same as (or different from) the pattern blocks?

Listening is difficult for kindergartners, and when every student shares what he or she did, their attention may wander. One way to vary these "sharing" discussions is by asking a few students to share what they did with a material and then ask others to think about how what they did was similar to what was just shared. For example:

Charlotte just told us that she built a castle using the Geoblocks. Raise you hand if you built castle or another kind of building. What kind of building did you build? Who made something with the Geoblocks that was *not* a building? Tell us about that.

Choice Time is an opportunity for students to work on a variety of activities that focus on similar mathematical content. In the kindergarten *Investigations* curriculum, Choice Time is a regular feature that follows each whole-group Focus Time. The activities in Choice Time are not sequential; as students move among them, they continually revisit the important concepts and ideas they are learning in that unit. Many Choice Time activities are designed with the intent that students will work on them more than once. As they play a game a second or third time, use a material over and over again, or solve many similar problems, students are able to refine their strategies, see a variety of approaches, and bring new knowledge to familiar experiences.

Scheduling Choice Time

Scheduling of the suggested Choice Time activities will depend on the structure of your classroom day. Many kindergarten teachers already have some type of "activity time" built into their daily schedule, and the Choice Time activities described in each investigation can easily be presented during these times. Some classrooms have a designated math time once a day or at least three or four times a week. In these cases you might spend one or two math times on a Focus Time activity, followed by five to seven days of Choice Time during math, with students choosing among three or four activities. New activities can be added every few days.

Setting Up the Choices

Many kindergarten teachers set up the Choice Time activities at centers or stations around the room. At each center, students will find the materials needed to complete the activity. Other teachers prefer to keep materials stored in a central location; students then take the materials they need to a designated workplace. In either case, materials should be readily accessible. When choosing an arrangement, you may need to experiment with a few different structures before finding the setup that works best for you and your students.

We suggest that you limit the number of students doing a Choice Time activity at any one time. In many cases, the quantity of materials available establishes the limit. Even if this is not the case, limiting the number is advisable because it gives students the opportunity to work in smaller groups. It also gives them a chance to do some choices more than once.

In the quantity of materials specified for each Choice Time activity, "per pair" refers to the number of students who will be doing that activity at the same time (usually not the entire class). You can plan the actual quantity needed for your class once you decide how many other activities will be available at the same time.

Many kindergarten teachers use some form of chart or Choice Board that tells which activities are available and for how many students. This organizer can be as simple as a list of the activities on chart paper, each activity identified with a little sketch. Ideas for pictures to help identify each different activity are found with the blackline masters for each kindergarten unit.

In some classrooms, teachers make permanent Choice Boards by attaching small hooks or Velcro strips onto a large board or heavy cardboard. The choices are written on individual strips and hung on the board. Next to each choice are additional hooks or Velcro pieces that indicate the number of students who can be working at that activity. Students each have a small name tag that they are responsible for moving around the Choice Board as they proceed from activity to activity.

Introducing New Choices

Choice Time activities are suggested at the end of each Focus Time. Plan to introduce these gradually, over a few days, rather than all at once on the same day. Often two or three of the choices will be familiar to students already, either because they are a direct extension of the Focus Time activity or because they are continuing from a previous investigation. On the first day of

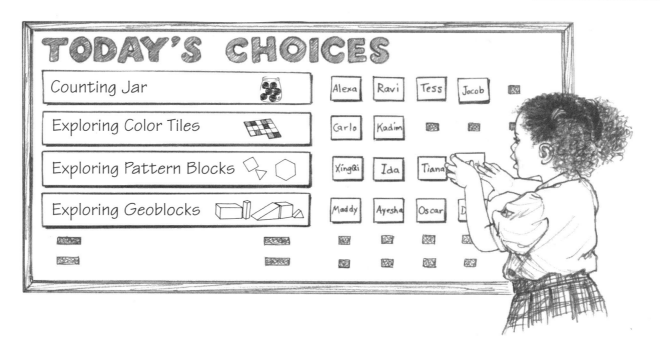

Choice Time, you might begin with the familiar activities and perhaps introduce one new activity. On subsequent days, one or two new activities can be introduced to students as you get them started on their Choice Time work. Most teachers find it both more efficient and more effective to introduce activities to the whole class at once.

Managing Choice Time

During the first weeks of Choice Time, you will need to take an active role in helping students learn the routine, your expectations, and how to plan what they do. We do not recommend organizing students into groups and circulating the groups every 15–20 minutes. For some students, this set time may be too long to spend at an activity; others may have only begun to explore the activity when it's time t~~~~~~

suggest that they make a different first choice and do the favorite activity as a second choice.

When a new choice is introduced, many students want to do it first. Initially you will need to give lots of reassurance that every student will have the chance to try each choice.

As students become more familiar with the Choice Time routine and the classroom structure, they will come to trust that activities are available for many days at a time.

For some activities, students will have a "product" to save or share. Some teachers provide folders where students can keep their work for each unit. Other teachers collect students' work in a central ~~~~~~ it in individual student ~~~~~~ many of the products ~~~~~~ of paper. Instead, students ~~~~~~ structions out of pattern ~~~~~~ bes, drawing graphs ~~~~~~ paper, and creating ~~~~~~ paper.

Continued on next page

For some activities, such as the counting games they play again and again, there may be no actual "product." For this reason, some teachers take photographs or jot down short anecdotal observations to record the work of their kindergarten students.

During the second half of the year, or when students seem very comfortable with Choice Time, you might consider asking them to keep track of the choices they have completed. This can be set up in one of these ways:

- Students each have a blank sheet of paper. When they have completed an activity, they record its name or picture on the paper.

- Post a sheet of lined paper at each station, or a sheet for each choice at the front of the room. At the top of the sheet, write the name of one activity with the corresponding picture. When students have completed an activity, they print their name on the appropriate sheet.

Some teachers keep a date stamp at each station or at the front of the room, making it easy for students to record the date as well. As they complete each choice, students place in a designated spot any work they have done during that activity.

In addition to learning about how to make choices and how to work productively on their own, students should be expected to take responsibility for cleaning up and returning materials to their appropriate storage locations. This requires a certain amount of organization on the part of the teacher—making sure storage bins are clearly labeled, and offering some instruction about how to clean up and how to care for the various materials. Giving students a "5 minutes until cleanup" warning before the end of any Choice Time session allows students to finish what they are working on and prepare for the upcoming transition.

At the end of a Choice Time, spend a few minutes discussing with students what went smoothly, what sorts of issues arose and how they were resolved, and what students enjoyed or found difficult. Encourage students to be involved in the process of finding solutions to problems that come up in the classroom. In doing so, they take some responsibility for their own behavior and become involved with establishing classroom policies.

Observing and Working with Students

During the initial weeks of Choice Time, much of your time will be spent in classroom management, circulating around the room, helping students get settled into activities, and monitoring the process of making choices and moving from one activity to another. Once routines are familiar and well established, however, students will become more independent and responsible for their own work. At this point, you will have time to observe and listen to students while they work. You might plan to meet with individual students, pairs, or small groups that need help; you might focus on students you haven't had a chance to observe before; or you might do individual assessments. The section About Assessment (p. I-8) explains the importance of this type of observation in the kindergarten curriculum and offers some suggestions for recording and using your observations.

Supporting Students' Free Play

Teacher Note

When students are first introduced to manipulative materials, they make a wide variety of choices about how to use them. Many students are able to set themselves tasks and successfully create something that they are pleased with. However, while some students dive right in, others need some support and structure to help them take their first steps. When students are hesitant, help them notice what their classmates are doing. You might encourage any of the following common approaches.

Making Patterns The pattern blocks, with their built-in geometric relationships, naturally lead to making pattern sequences or symmetrical designs. Some students use pattern blocks on their edges to make a "wall" in a certain pattern, for example, hexagon, triangle, hexagon, triangle, hexagon, triangle. Others make flat patterns, often working outward from a central hexagon.

Starting with a hexagon is something you might suggest to students who are stuck. Making a "wall" around a "garden" (which can be a piece of paper) is another possibility to suggest. Some students will become intrigued with creating symmetrical or balanced designs. This is a good opportunity to introduce the idea of symmetry: "Your design is *symmetrical*. It's the same on this side and on this side."

Making Buildings Sometimes students will start with an idea and carry it through: "I'm going to build a castle." Other times, they will just start building and then notice that their construction reminds them of something: "It looks like a Chinese temple. Now I'm going to make the steps."

Sometimes students working independently will join their separate buildings into one structure: "I made this part and Henry made this part of it, and we decided to put it together. This part's the museum and this part is the living room, and the rest is everything else." Encouraging this kind of connecting of separate structures can also help when you are dealing with limited quantities of materials.

Accumulating Lots of Blocks or Cubes Young students love to accumulate things. One building approach that reflects this love is to enclose space in some way and then collect other blocks inside the enclosure: "This is the treasure room and these are the treasure." And: "This is a junkyard and this is where they store the tires, and this is where they have things that don't work any more, and these are the flags that are hung up."

Students like to make long trains or snakes with the cubes, or to make tall towers. Counting can come up with any of these materials, but it is especially likely with the interlocking cubes. Questions such as these lead to a focus on counting: "How tall can you make it before it breaks? Can you make a train as long as the table? How many cubes did you use?"

Sharing Good Ideas It's impossible to predict what will come up in your class, but be alert to ideas from your students that others in the class might enjoy. Sometimes these ideas sweep through the class without any help from you. For example, in one class, a student started using the interlocking cubes to make her initials. Soon other children were trying to make their own initials. The teacher engaged them in conversation about which letters were difficult and why. In another classroom, students (and the teacher) became intrigued with ways in which they could balance some of the Geoblocks on each other.

Establishing Constraints It helps some students to get started if you set them a small problem with some constraint. For example, suggest that they use a certain number of blocks or cubes. You can adjust the numbers for different students. For example:

Make a design with 12 pattern blocks.

Make a building with 20 Geoblocks.

You can also ask them to make a building or pattern that fits on a standard sheet of paper. Using paper as a mat helps students contain their work and limits the number of blocks or cubes a single student can use.

Talking About Pattern Blocks and Geoblocks

As you observe students working with pattern blocks and Geoblocks, you can learn a lot about what they notice about two- and three-dimensional shapes: what characteristics they attend to, what relationships they recognize, and what distinctions they make. For example, you might hear students say things like this:

"Hand me that little square block."

"I'm using diamonds all around the edge."

"I need more yellow ones."

"We need two more of those big long ones."

"I need to find another roof one."

Since all pattern blocks of the same color are the same shape, it is very natural for students to identify them by color. This is fine, and should not be discouraged. At the same time, we want students to become familiar with and eventually use correct geometric terms for different shapes.

At this age, students will not use many conventional mathematical terms. For example, they will probably not know that a blue pattern block is a *rhombus* or *parallelogram*, but may instead use the everyday term *diamond*. They are likely to know some geometric names, such as *square*, or even *triangle*, but may apply these incorrectly. For example, when using the Geoblocks, they might call a cube a *square* or call a triangle a *rectangle*.

As you talk with students, use the same terms they are using, but help them develop their language by asking questions or making comments that challenge them to be clearer and more precise. The following interactions demonstrate how you might do this. In the first example, the teacher calls attention to the idea that even though blue and tan pattern blocks are not identical in shape, both can be described by the same shape name.

Shanique: I'm making a path with the diamonds.

Are you using all blue diamonds, or are you going to use some of the tan diamonds?

In a similar manner, the teacher points out to another student that the cubes ("square ones") in the Geoblock set come in several sizes.

Ravi: I'm using the square ones to build a wall.

There are lots of Geoblocks like that. Are you going to use the tiny square ones or the bigger ones?

You can also introduce conventional mathematical names for two- and three-dimensional shapes, so that students hear these terms used in context. For example, here the teacher introduces the term *hexagon* for the yellow pattern block and *rhombus* for the blue one.

Felipe: When I put three blue ones on top of the yellow one, they just fit.

Felipe noticed that three of these blue rhombus shapes can fit right on top of the hexagon. Did anyone notice any other pieces that can fit right on the hexagon?

In an interaction at the Geoblock station, the teacher introduces the term *cubes*.

Tiana: I need more tiny boxes for the top of my castle.

Tiana is looking for tiny cubes. See how she's using them on her castle? Does anyone have some of the smallest cubes that Tiana could use?

Students are not expected to use the geometric terms in kindergarten. They will begin to learn them naturally, as they learn other vocabulary, by hearing them used correctly in context. Throughout the elementary grades, students will have many experiences in classifying, describing, and defining shapes of both two and three dimensions.

Flowers, Dancers, and Pattern Block Walls

Students vary in the amount of structure and direction they need as they freely explore materials. Asking questions can be an effective way of guiding and structuring a free exploration experience for some students. This can extend their thinking about a particular material and lead them into new ways of using it. When students work with a partner or small group, they benefit from observing how others use materials. Inviting students to share their constructions and designs is a natural way to exchange ideas.

The following dialogue occurred early in the year during a free exploration Choice Time. The teacher joins a small group of students working with pattern blocks and asks them to tell her about their constructions.

Kylie: I have a flower. See, the yellow one is the middle, and then the flower part is all around with the blue. And then the green triangles are the stem part.

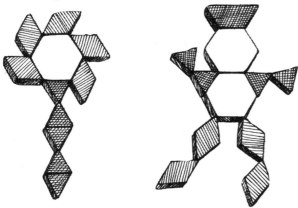

Gabriela: Mine is a person. Here is her hat. It's red. And then she sort of looks like she is dancing, because these ones, these blue diamonds are her legs.

Yes, you made her legs using the blue rhombus shapes, and it does look like she is dancing.

Kylie: And you used green triangles just like me. But you made her arms and I made a stem.

Carlo: Stop shaking the table! I don't want my wall to fall down.

Some of you have decided to use the pattern blocks flat on the table and some of you have used them to build up, sort of like blocks. It is harder to keep them in place when they're on their edges the way Carlo has them. Carlo, can you tell me about your wall?

Carlo: Well, it goes yellow, red, yellow, red, yellow, red and then it switches to yellow, blue, yellow, blue. See, they sort of fit together, right next to each other.

Yes, I see that the side of the red trapezoid fits right into the side of the yellow hexagon. And the side of the blue rhombus also fits into the side of the hexagon. I wonder what other blocks will fit exactly together so that you can make that kind of wall?

The conversation is interrupted by some commotion at another table. Three students are building elaborate constructions using pattern blocks. Two are being silly, sliding blocks back and forth across the table. The teacher addresses these two students.

Ravi and Tess, I remember that the other day you were interested in trying to make a design that would cover a piece of drawing paper, but time ran out and you didn't have a chance to do it. Would you be interested in trying to work on that problem now?

Ravi: Yeah, let's do that.

Tess: No, I don't want to. I want to keep doing this. *[She slides another block across the table.]*

Ravi, you can get a piece of paper from the art shelf. Tess, you'll have to make a choice about what you want to do. Sliding blocks is not one of the choices of how to use the pattern blocks. If you want to use the blocks today, you'll have to use them in a responsible way. If not, you'll need to leave this activity and make a new choice.

Counting Jar

Focus Time

Counting Jar (p. 26)

Counting Jar is a suggested ongoing classroom routine that focuses on counting and representing quantities. The activity has three steps: students count the number of items in a jar, find a way to show that information using numbers or pictures, and then count out their own set that contains an equivalent number of another object.

Choice Time

Counting Jar (p. 32)

Students get a chance to visit the Counting Jar independently to count a new set of objects, to record their count on the class chart, and to create a collection of the same number of a different object on a paper plate.

Continuing from Investigation 1

Exploring Color Tiles (p. 12)

Exploring Pattern Blocks (p. 14)

Exploring Geoblocks (p. 16)

Mathematical Emphasis

- Counting a set of objects
- Creating a set of a given size
- Recording numerical information
- Exploring materials that will be used in this unit and throughout the curriculum

Teacher Support

Teacher Notes

From the Classroom: Getting Started (p. 34)

Counting Is More Than 1, 2, 3 (p. 36)

Observing Students As They Count (p. 37)

Materials As Tools for Learning (p. 38)

Dialogue Box

You Could Use Dots (p. 39)

What to Plan Ahead of Time

Focus Time Materials

Counting Jar

- *Mouse Count* by Ellen Stoll Walsh (Harcourt Brace Jovanovich, 1991), or similar counting book (optional)
- A clear plastic jar or container, at least 6 inches tall and 4–5 inches in diameter, for the Counting Jar
- Medium-sized objects of the same type to put in the Counting Jar, such as golf or table-tennis balls, walnuts, small blocks, spools of thread: from 5 to 12 of each type
- A variety of countable materials, such as interlocking cubes, color tiles, teddy bear counters, buttons, keys, pebbles, or pennies
- Index cards or paper cut to 4 by 6 inches: several for demonstration
- Chart paper for a Counting Jar recording chart (see p. 68 for a description and illustration)

Choice Time Materials

Counting Jar

- Counting Jar from Focus Time, with a new set of objects inside
- Prepared recording sheet and 4-by-6-inch cards or paper: 1 per student, plus extras
- Paper plates: 1 per student
- Collections of countable materials

Exploring Color Tiles

- Color tiles: 1 bucket per 8–10 students, with scoops
- One-inch grid paper, paper squares cut from construction paper, glue sticks, unlined paper, and coloring materials (optional)

Exploring Pattern Blocks

- Pattern blocks: 1 bucket per 4–6 students, with scoops
- Paper pattern blocks, glue sticks (optional)
- Unlined paper and coloring materials, available

Exploring Geoblocks

- Geoblocks: 1 or 2 sets per classroom, divided into smaller sets
- Other classroom sets of building blocks (optional)
- Unlined paper and drawing materials, available

Focus Time

Counting Jar

What Happens

After reading a book about counting to 10, students count the items in the class Counting Jar to determine how many there are. They discuss ways of showing that information using pictures or numbers. They then create another collection of objects that has the same number of items in it. Their work focuses on:

- counting a set of objects
- creating a set of a given size
- recording numerical information

Materials and Preparation

- Obtain a copy of *Mouse Count* by Ellen Stoll Walsh (Harcourt Brace Jovanovich, 1991), in big book form if possible (optional).
- In the Counting Jar, place a manageable number of interesting objects to be counted, such as 5 tennis balls, 6 golf balls, 8 wooden cubes, or 9 teddy bear counters. For this introduction, use objects that are large enough for all students to see in whole-group meeting.
- Set up your prepared recording chart for the Counting Jar, filling in the name of the objects in the jar.
- Have a number of 4-by-6-inch cards or slips of paper ready to model ways of recording the students' counts.
- Have available several paper plates and a variety of smaller countable materials (interlocking cubes, color tiles, buttons, keys, pebbles, or pennies).

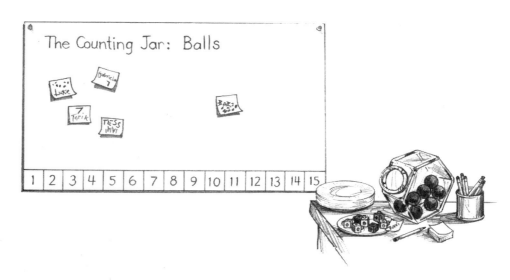

Mouse Count

Begin this activity by asking students to think about times we use counting. If you have done the Investigation 1 Focus Time activity, Attendance, students will have had at least one experience with counting in school.

Each morning when you arrive at school, we count the number of people who are here in our class. I need to know how many students are in school so that [I can make sure we have enough snack for everyone, or, I'll know how many students are in our group when we go out to recess]. So, the first thing we do each day is *count* you. What are some other times that you have counted, or you have seen someone else count?

After students have shared their ideas, introduce the book *Mouse Count*. If you do not have a copy of this book or another suitable counting book, simply skip to the next activity to introduce the Counting Jar.

Mouse Count tells the story of hungry snake who finds ten mice and counts them as he drops them into a jar to save for dinner. The clever mice find a way to escape from the jar and uncount themselves as they run back home.

As you read the story, pause occasionally for students to count how many mice the snake has captured in the jar. After one student counts, double-check by having the class count aloud as you point to each mouse on the page.

After reading the story, discuss one or two of the following questions:

How did the mice outsmart the snake?

When the jar had all 10 mice in it, do you think there was enough room for one more mouse? If the snake did add one more mouse, how many mice would have been in the jar?

How did the mice work together to escape from the snake?

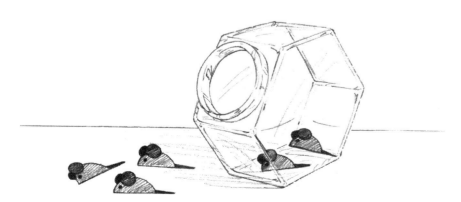

Counting and Showing the Count

Note: For more information about the Counting Jar, including variations you can introduce throughout the year, see the section About Classroom Routines: Counting Jar (p. 68). In particular, read the explanation of why the task of estimation is not part of the basic activity, and how it can be included later in the year as students become more familiar with quantities and the numbers that represent them.

Show students the Counting Jar with objects inside.

This is a special kind of jar we'll be using all year. It's called a Counting Jar. What do you think we will do with it?

If you have just read *Mouse Count,* students are likely to relate your jar to the one that the snake filled with mice. After students have shared their ideas, ask them how they could find out how many items are in the jar. Some students might suggest counting the objects by taking them out of the jar, while others might count just by looking inside the jar. This may depend on the objects you have chosen and how many are in the jar. Ask volunteers to demonstrate how they would count the objects. Encourage the students to see what they notice about each person's strategy for counting.

Early in the year, students may make a variety of mistakes as they count and ultimately not agree on how many items are in the jar. When discrepancies arise, focus group discussion on strategies for counting and for keeping track of or organizing the count, rather than on which person counted correctly. Involve students in thinking about reasons for the differences and reasons for losing count. Also talk about double-checking as a useful and important tool in counting accurately. Refer to the **Teacher Notes**, Counting Is More Than 1, 2, 3 (p. 36) and Observing Students as They Count (p. 37), for more on kindergarten students and counting.

After you count what's in the Counting Jar, each one of you is going to put your answer on this chart. You'll have a pencil and a little card to use for this. Suppose I counted six balls in the jar. How could I show on my paper that there are six balls in the jar? Who can think of a way? . . . Does anyone have a different idea?

With the class, brainstorm ideas about how to convey the information. Model each idea students suggest on a 4-by-6-inch card or slip of paper. Post each model on the prepared recording chart.

Some students might suggest using pictures or slash marks to show the six objects; others might suggest using a numeral. Some might suggest a numeral, but not know how to write it. Point out the number line on the chart and any numbers elsewhere in the room, such as on the calendar, that students can use for reference.

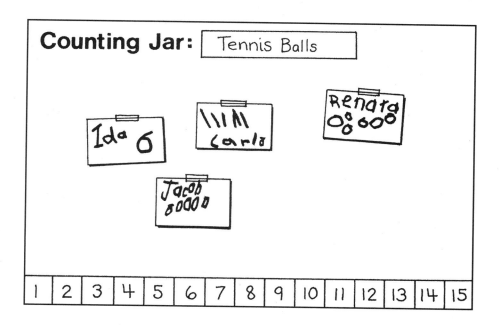

Make clear to the class that you are not looking for a single method of recording the counts. Students need to experience the idea that information can be recorded in different ways for use at a later time. The **Dialogue Box**, You Could Use Dots (p. 39), demonstrates how one class talked about recording their counts for the Counting Jar.

Counting Out a New Set

I counted six balls in the Counting Jar. Now we're going to make another collection of six things, to match the number I found in the jar.

Creating another set of objects that has the same quantity as the jar maximizes the counting experience students get from this activity. Point out the sets of countable objects you have assembled, and ask for two or three volunteers to each choose a different material and count out six objects. Give each student a paper plate for their collection and display these plates where everyone can see them. To involve more students, ask for volunteers to double-check the amount in each collection.

So now we have lots of different collections of six objects. There were six balls in the Counting Jar, and here on the plates we have [six buttons, and six cubes, and six pennies]. And here [point to the recording chart] **are some different ways to use pictures or numbers to show that there are six.**

Explain that the Counting Jar will be an activity they will be doing during Choice Time, and throughout the school year.

Before Choice Time, I'm going to put a different set in the Counting Jar. When you visit this station, your job will be to find out how many things are in the jar. After you have counted what's in the jar, find a way to show that information using numbers or pictures, and post your answer on the chart. Be sure your name is on your answer.

Briefly remind students of the different ways suggested earlier for showing the number of objects in the jar.

After you have put your count on the chart, choose something else—the tiles, the cubes, the buttons, anything in these tubs—to make a group with the same number as the jar. So, if the jar has six things in it, you would make another group of six things. Put your new collection on a paper plate. We'll put your name on the plate so we'll know which one is yours.

It is hard to observe all students as they count and create sets, but with the chart and the plates, you can save their work until you have more time to look it over. In the meantime, students enjoy looking at each other's collections and answers on the chart, and debating how many objects are in the jar each time.

Sharing How We Counted

Students will be visiting the Counting Jar during Choice Time while they also continue to explore materials at the other stations. Keep an eye on the recording chart, and when most of the students have finished with the Counting Jar, plan a short discussion.

Because there is a "right answer" to this problem, students are likely to be very excited about knowing what the answer is. However, the emphasis should not be on the answer, or who was right and who was wrong, since students can come up with the correct answer but arrive at it by miscounting. Focusing instead on the different ways students recorded the number of objects in the jar, or the strategies they used for counting, can help reduce any competition.

I noticed that some people used a picture of the cubes to show how many were in the jar. Raise your hand if you drew pictures of the things in the jar. . . . Some other people used lines to show how many. Who used lines?

And some people used numbers. How many of you wrote numbers? These are all good ways of showing the number of objects in the Counting Jar.

When I was watching you count the things in the jar, I noticed that people did it in different ways. Some of you took out one object at a time as you counted. Raise your hand if you did that. . . . Did anyone count the objects in a different way?

Focus Time Follow-Up

Four Choices During Choice Time, students may visit the Counting Jar to repeat independently the activity introduced during Focus Time. In addition, they may continue with the three Choice Time activities from the previous investigation.

 **Choice Time**

Decide whether you want all students to visit the Counting Jar, or only those who choose to. Since not all students will be able to work on this activity at the same time or within the same day, you'll need to leave the Counting Jar out for several days and perhaps at other times during the school day. Some teachers have the Counting Jar available to students as they enter the classroom in the morning as well as during any free activity times in the daily schedule.

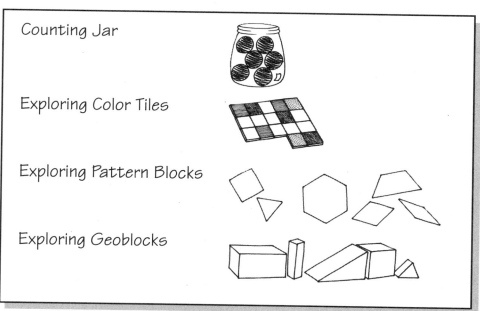

Choice Time

Counting Jar

What Happens

Students count a new set of items in the Counting Jar to determine how many there are. They record that information using pictures or numbers, then create another collection of objects with the same number of items in it. Their work focuses on:

■ counting a set of objects
■ creating a set of a given size
■ recording numerical information

Materials and Preparation

■ Place a new set of materials in the Counting Jar, choosing a number that is suitable for most students in your class. While it may seem exciting to put large numbers of objects in the jar, we strongly recommend somewhere between 5 and 12, a quantity that is both manageable and understandable to kindergartners.

■ Set up the recording chart for the Counting Jar, with a stack of 4-by-6-inch cards or slips of paper, at least 1 per student, for recording the counts.

■ Provide a supply of paper plates, 1 per student, with students' names on them, along with tubs of countable materials, such as interlocking cubes, color tiles, teddy bear counters, buttons, keys, or pennies.

Activity

After the Focus Time activity, Counting Jar, students will need little introduction to this choice. Show them where you have set up the jar.

Who can remind us what we do with this special Counting Jar?

Explain that the activity is the same, only now there is a different type of object, or a different amount, in the jar. Students count the items in the jar, then record their total and post it on the recording chart. As necessary, call attention to this chart and ask students to remember some strategies they thought of for recording their counts during Focus Time.

Remind students that after they have counted the objects in the jar and recorded their count, they then create another set of objects with the same quantity as in the jar, placing the new collection on a paper plate.

Observing the Students

As students work through the three parts of this activity, observe to get a sense of how comfortable they are with the tasks.

■ Do students know the sequence of number names? Do they forget or mix the order of some of the numbers? Which ones?

Some students will not yet have a solid grasp of the number sequence. Encourage those who get lost in the sequence of numbers to count again from the beginning, to count on from where you leave off, to count with you, or to repeat the number after you as you count. Students learn the sequence and how to count by having repeated chances to count and to hear others count.

■ Do students have a system for counting the objects in the jar? Do they remove one object at a time? Do they dump out the contents and randomly count? Do they organize them in some way? Do they touch or move each item as they count it? Do they empty the jar, then put one object at a time back in the jar as they count? Do they double-check their count?

■ How do students record the number of objects they think are in the jar? Do they use pictures to represent the objects? Do they use numbers? Do they have a strategy for figuring out how to write a particular number? Do they just know how some numbers look? Do they refer to the number line, calendar, or other written numerals?

■ How do students create a new set of objects with the same amount as the jar? Do they count out the amount? Do they compare their set in any way to the set in the jar by matching the items one to one to make an equivalent set? Do they double-check their counts?

If students are having difficulty making an equivalent set, suggest that they try matching one object to each object in the jar.

When most of the students have visited the Counting Jar, call them together to talk briefly about what they found out. Refer to the activity Sharing How We Counted (p. 30) for some tips on handling this discussion.

Teacher Note > *Getting Started*

At the beginning of the school year, I'm always a bit shocked at how young and inexperienced my new kindergarten students are. I still have in my memory those kindergartners that I said good-bye to in June—those kindergartners who knew how to make choices about what to work on; those kindergartners who knew the expectations for using materials and how to clean up and put them away when Choice Time was over; those kindergartners who could share their ideas at a class meeting. That was June and this is September—and after only two days, I remembered the work of the first few months of school: establishing the routines and establishing the expectations that turn chaos and confusion into a productive, self-directed mathematical community.

The Classroom Routines We are now in our third week of school and our second week of this unit. The introduction of the first two classroom routines went quite smoothly. We do Attendance each morning, and first determine how many are in school by using a counting method suggested by a student. Then we double-check this count by counting off—and after only one week, my students seem to understand the process. While many in this class seem to know the rote counting sequence up to 26 [the number in the class], only a handful seem to understand what the number they say actually means. I know from past experience that this understanding develops over time and through repeated opportunities to count in different contexts.

The Counting Jar activity seems like an excellent counting experience. In the past I have had an Estimating Jar, a similar activity in which students begin by guessing how many items I have placed in the jar. I initially questioned the absence of estimation in this Counting Jar activity, but when I really thought about it, I realized that in order to estimate successfully, a person needs a sense of quantity and a sense of what would be a reasonable quantity. The Counting Jar offers students both of those experiences. So I'll try this and see what happens.

I've placed the Counting Jar on a low bookshelf that holds a number of our math manipulatives. My expectation is that it will be available to students throughout the day. Every two or three days, during one of our class meetings, we empty the contents of the jar, count them, and look at the equivalent collections students have made. One thing that has surprised me is that students don't visit this activity just once. I've seen at least seven or eight students count the same contents and then make another collection two and even three times. My initial reaction was "No, this is an activity that you do once." But after thinking about it, isn't this the way students learn about counting—*by counting?* Even though it may seem boring to an adult to count the same amount in the jar more than once (especially such a small amount), this just isn't the case for 5- and 6-year-olds.

Choice Time While the Attendance routine and the Counting Jar are off to a successful start, Choice Time is a different story. This year I have an extended-day kindergarten, with students in school from 8:30 A.M. to 1:00 P.M., so I decided to have a separate Math Time each day. Math Time is a 45-minute period that usually takes place right after our morning meeting. Since I have always had an activity time, I thought that my Math Time would be similar in structure. I would have four or five activities for student to choose from, each for about four to six students, depending on the available materials and space.

When I first started Math Time, I decided that since students were just exploring materials and not really doing any specific activity, I would introduce all three materials—pattern blocks, color tiles, and Geoblocks—on the same day. I organized the materials at six centers, two for each material, and explained that students could use whatever material they wanted to, as long as there was a space for them at the table. After three days of chaos, I could see that my introduction of Math Time was too casual. Many of the students seemed overwhelmed. They were interested and excited by the materials, but were unsure about how to use them or even how to get a turn with them.

On the fourth day, I decided to begin again and reintroduce Math Time. I chose only two of the materials, pattern blocks and Geoblocks. I divided the pattern blocks into four sets and the Geoblocks into three sets, storing each set in a shoe box. I placed each set at a table and also used the rugs in the meeting area and in the block area since I don't have enough tables in my room to accommodate so many stations. At each table I placed four chairs; this would signal students as to how many could use that material at any one time.

During our morning meeting, I showed the class the pattern blocks and the Geoblocks and asked for ideas about what they could do with them. I was amazed at how many ideas they had, given that the last three days had seemed so chaotic. As a class, we discussed how to take care of each material and how to clean up your working space when you are finished. Once again, my students seemed to have good ideas about how to work responsibly and take care of materials. (I know from experience, though, that kindergartners can *talk* about how to clean up, but when faced with the actual task, they are less interested!)

To help the children make choices about where to start, I turned to the Choice Board I always use for activity time. This is a large rectangular board arrayed with cup hooks. Down the left side of the board, I hang a tag for each available activity. The tag usually has a word (e.g., Pattern Blocks) and a picture. I put each tag next to a specific number of hooks, to indicate how many children can be in that area or at that activity. By looking at the board, the children know what activities are open and how many of them can be there. Each student has a personal "choice tag" that they hang next to an activity when they are working there. As they move from activity to activity, they are responsible for moving their tag. This system works well during our general activity time, so I figured why not use it during Math Time, too. I hung four Pattern Block tags, three Geoblock tags, and one Counting Jar tag— one tag for each station. I hung each Pattern Block and Geoblock tag next to four hooks, and the Counting Jar tag next to two hooks.

My students were very excited about having the Choice Board for Math Time. It was already somewhat familiar to them since they had been using it for activity time during the first two weeks of school. With this preparation, Math Time went more smoothly than it had in the previous three days. More students seemed engaged with the materials. I spent most of my time helping students make transitions into a choice rather than watching their work, but I know from years past that during the first couple of months, I usually don't have a lot of time to observe or work with individual students. Instead, most of my energy is directed at helping my students become familiar with classroom routines and how the classroom works.

Counting is the basis for understanding our number system and for almost all the number work in the primary grades. It involves more than just knowing the number names, their sequence, and how to write each numeral. While it may seem simple, counting is actually quite complex and involves the interplay between the following skills and concepts.

Rote Counting Students need to know the number names and their order by rote; they learn this sequence by hearing others count and by counting themselves. However, just as saying the alphabet does not indicate that a student can use written language, being able to say "one, two, three, four, five, six, seven, eight, nine, ten" does not necessarily indicate that students know what those counting words mean. Students also need to use numbers in meaningful ways if they are to build an understanding of quantity and number relationships.

One-to-One Correspondence To count accurately, a student must know that one number name stands for one object that is counted. Often, when young children first begin to count, they do not connect the numbers in the "counting song" to the objects they are counting. Children learn about one-to-one correspondence through repeated opportunities to count sets of objects and to watch others as they count. One-to-one correspondence develops over time, with students first counting small groups of objects (up to five or six) accurately, and eventually larger groups.

Keeping Track Another important part of counting accurately is being able to keep track of what has been counted and what still remains to be counted. As students first begin to count sets of objects, they often count some objects more than once and skip other objects altogether. Students develop strategies for organizing and keeping track of a count as they realize the need and as they see others use such strategies.

Connecting Numbers to Quantities We use numbers both to count a set of objects and to describe the quantity of those objects. Many young students are still coordinating these two aspects of number—the *ordinal* sequence of the numbers with the *cardinal* meaning of those numbers. In other words, we get to 5 by counting in order, 1, 2, 3, 4, 5. In this sequence, 4 comes after 3, and 5 comes after 4. Understanding this aspect of number is connected to the one-to-one correspondence between the numbers we say and the objects we are counting. However, being able to count accurately using this ordinal sequence is not the same as knowing that when we are finished counting, the final number in our sequence tells the quantity of the things we have counted.

Conservation Conservation of number involves understanding that three is always three, whether it's three objects pushed or linked together, three objects spread apart in a line, or some other formation. As students learn to count, you will see many who do not yet understand this idea. They think that the larger the arrangement of objects, the more objects there are. Being able to conserve quantity is not a skill that can be taught; it is a cognitive process that develops as children grow and develop. This unit provides many opportunities for kindergartners to bump up against this important developmental milestone.

Counting by Groups Counting a set of objects by equal groups, such as 2's, requires that each of the steps mentioned above happens again, at a different level. First, students need to know the 2's sequence (2, 4, 6, 8 . . .) by rote. They need to realize that one number in this count represents two objects, and that each time they say a number they are adding another group of two to their count. Keeping track while counting by groups becomes a more complex task as well. Students begin to explore counting by groups in the data unit *Counting Ourselves and Others* as they count the number of eyes in their class (counting by 2's). However, most students will not count by groups in a meaningful way until first or second grade.

Observing Students As They Count

In kindergarten, you can expect to see a wide range of number skills within your class. Students in the same class can vary considerably in age and in their previous experience with numbers and counting.

Your students will have many opportunities to count and use numbers in this unit and throughout the year. You can learn a lot about what your students understand by observing them. Listen to students as they talk with each other. Observe them as they count orally, as they count objects, and as they use numerals to record. Ask them about their thinking. You may observe some of the following:

Counting Orally By the end of the year, most kindergarten students will have learned to count by rote up to 10 and beyond, with some able to count as high as 100. Many will be able to count orally much higher than they can count objects. For many students who have learned the internal counting pattern or sequence (1, 2, 3 . . . 21, 22, 23 . . .), the "bridge" numbers into the next decade (such as 19, 20, or 29, 30) remain difficult. You may hear children count "twenty-eight, twenty-nine, twenty-ten." Just as the young child who says "I runned away" understands something about the regularities of the English language, the student who says "twenty-ten" understands something about the regularity of counting quantities. Students will gradually learn the bridge numbers through repeated experiences with counting and listening to the counting sequence.

Counting Quantities Most kindergartners will end the year with a grasp of *quantities* up to 10 or so. Some students may accurately count quantities above 10 or even 20; others may not consistently count quantities up to 5 or 6. Some students may be inconsistent—successful one time, having difficulty the next. Even when students can accurately count the objects in a set, they may not know that the last number they said also describes the number of objects in the set.

You may observe students who successfully count a set of cubes, but have to go back and recount the set to answer the question, "How many cubes are there?" These students have not yet made the connection of the counting numbers with the quantity of objects in a set. Students develop their understanding of quantity through repeated experiences organizing and counting sets of objects. In kindergarten, many of the activities that focus on quantity can be adjusted so that students are working at a level of challenge appropriate for them.

Organizing a Count Some students may be able to count objects they can pick up, move around, and organize with far more accuracy than they can count static objects, such as pictures of things on a page. You may observe some students who can count objects correctly when the group is organized for them, but you'll see others who have trouble organizing or keeping track of objects themselves. They will need many and varied experiences with counting to develop techniques for counting accurately and for keeping track of what they are counting.

Writing Numbers Knowing how to write numerals is not directly related to counting and understanding quantity; however, it is useful for representing a quantity that has been counted. Young students who are learning how to write numerals frequently reverse numbers or digits. Often this is not a mathematical problem but a matter of experience. Students need many opportunities to see how numerals are formed and to practice writing them. They should gain this experience by using numbers to record mathematical information, such as the number of students in school today or the number of objects in the counting jar. Numeral formation is related to letter formation; both are important in order to communicate in writing. We recommend that rote practice of numeral writing be part of handwriting instruction rather than mathematics.

Concrete materials are used throughout the *Investigations* curriculum as tools for learning. Students of all ages benefit from being able to use materials to model problems and explain their thinking.

The more available materials are, the more likely students are to use them. Having materials available means that they are readily accessible and that students are allowed to make decisions about which tools to use and when to use them. In much the same way that you choose the best tool to use for certain projects or tasks, students also should be encouraged to think about which material best meets their needs. To store manipulatives where they are easily accessible to the class, many teachers use plastic tubs or shoe boxes arranged on a bookshelf or along a windowsill. This storage can hold pattern blocks, Geoblocks, interlocking cubes, square tiles, counters such as buttons or bread tabs, and paper for student use.

It is important to encourage all students to use materials. If manipulatives are used only when someone is having difficulty, students can get the mistaken idea that using materials is a less sophisticated and less valued way of solving a problem. Encourage students to talk about how they used certain materials. They should see how different people, including the teacher, use a variety of materials in solving the same problem.

Introducing a New Material: Free Exploration
Students need time to explore a new material before using it in structured activities. By freely exploring a material, students will discover many of its important characteristics and will have some understanding of when it might make sense to use it. Although some free exploration should be done during regular math time, many teachers make materials available to students during free times or before or after school.

Each new material may present particular issues that you will want to discuss with your students. For example, to head off the natural tendency of some children to make guns with the interlocking cubes, you might establish a rule of "no weapons in the classroom." Some students like to build very tall structures with the Geoblocks. You may want to specify certain places where tall structures can be made—for example, on the floor in a particular corner—so that when they come crashing down, they are contained in that area.

Establishing Routines for Using Materials
Establish clear expectations about how materials will be used and cared for. Consider asking the students to suggest rules for how materials should and should not be used; they are often be more attentive to rules and policies that they have helped create.

Initially you may need to place buckets of materials close to students as they work. Gradually, students should be expected to decide what they need and get materials on their own.

Plan a cleanup routine at the end of each class. Making an announcement a few minutes before the end of a work period helps prepare students for the transition that is about to occur. You can then give students several minutes to return materials to their containers and double-check the floor for any stray materials. Most teachers find that establishing routines for using and caring for materials at the beginning of the year is well worth the time and effort.

You Could Use Dots

These students are brainstorming ways to record the number of balls in the Counting Jar. As each idea is suggested, the teacher models how to record the information on a new slip of paper, then tapes the slip onto their chart.

We have counted the balls in three different ways, and each time we figured out that there were seven balls in the jar. Suppose I wanted to write that information down on paper. Who has an idea about how I could show that there were seven balls on the jar?

Kadim: You could just write "7 balls."

Tess: Yeah, just write a 7.

Like this? *[The teacher writes "7 BALLS" on a slip of paper.]* I'm going to write your names on this paper since this was your idea. But I have a question for you. Suppose I didn't know how to write the number 7. How could I find out?

Alexa: You could ask me, because I know how to write numbers.

Kadim: Me, too!

You could ask a friend. Is there another way?

Carlo: You could look right there *[points to the number line that wraps around the meeting area]*. And find the 7. *[He touches each number as he counts]* 1, 2, 3, 4, 5, 6, 7.

The number line is a good place to find out how to write numbers. Is there anything else in the classroom that could help you?

Miyuki: The calendar has numbers.

Kylie: The chart has numbers on the bottom.

So one way you could write down how many things in the jar is by using a number. Are there any other ways to show how many? What if you didn't use numbers?

Ida: You could draw what's in the jar.

What would you draw this time?

Ida: I would draw some balls—like, you could use dots to show them.

So on another paper, I'll draw some circles to show the balls. And I'll write Ida's name on the paper to show it was her idea.

Kylie: You should draw seven of them.

Kylie, could you double-check to see if I have drawn the right number of balls?

Gabriela: You could make some lines like this. *[Gabriela comes to the front of the group and draws lines on a slip of paper. The teacher notices that she has drawn only six lines.]*

Gabriela, is there a way that you can double-check your work?

Gabriela: Umm, count? *[She counts the lines she has drawn and adds one more.]*

Why did you decide to add another line?

Gabriela: Because there should be seven lines for seven balls and I had six lines.

Brendan: I have a different way. You could use the stamps and make the number.

That's an idea I hadn't thought of. Should I put some of the stamps from the art table next to the Counting Jar? *[Students nod.]*

Kadim: Well, I'm going to use numbers.

Tiana: I'm going to draw balls, too, like Ida.

Many of you have the same idea about how to show the number of things in the Counting Jar. It's OK to use the same idea. Just be sure your name is on the paper you tape on the chart.

In this discussion, the teacher was able to get a sense of how different students might approach the task. She was particularly interested in Gabriela's solution of drawing lines to represent the balls, but when she drew only six lines, the teacher didn't know if she thought there were six objects in the jar or if she had miscounted the lines. By asking Gabriela to double-check her work, the teacher learned that in fact the girl had miscounted and was able to correct the information independently.

Calendar

Focus Time

Calendar (p. 42)

In this activity, the calendar is introduced as a tool for keeping track of events in time. Using the calendar is another practical situation that involves counting and offers daily practice with numbers. Thus, Calendar is suggested for use as an ongoing daily classroom routine in the kindergarten *Investigations* curriculum.

Choice Time

Exploring Interlocking Cubes (p. 48)

Continuing their exploration of materials, students engage in free play with interlocking cubes, a material that's useful for activities in pattern and counting, as well as for making three-dimensional constructions.

Continuing from Previous Investigations

Counting Jar (p. 32)

Exploring Materials (Teacher's Choice)

Mathematical Emphasis

- Developing a sense of time (days, weeks)
- Using the calendar as a tool for keeping track of time and events
- Counting on the calendar
- Connecting number names, numerals, and quantities
- Exploring materials that will be used throughout the curriculum

Teacher Support

Teacher Note

Encouraging Students to Think, Reason, and Share Ideas (p. 50)

Dialogue Boxes

Only Six More Days (p. 47)

What's a Calendar? (p. 51)

What to Plan Ahead of Time

Focus Time Materials

Calendar

- *Only Six More Days* by Marisabina Russo (Puffin Books, 1988) (optional)
- A calendar with removable numbers, such as a pocket calendar
- Cards, tags, or markers for highlighting special days on the calendar
- Several different types of calendars, such as a datebook, a whole-year wall calendar, and an appointment book

Choice Time Materials

Exploring Interlocking Cubes

- Interlocking cubes: class set
- Containers and scoops for the cubes

Exploring Materials (Teacher's Choice)

- Class sets of color tiles, pattern blocks, Geoblocks, or other materials, with scoops as needed
- Unlined paper and coloring materials, available

Counting Jar

- Counting Jar with a set of 5–12 items (e.g., cubes, balls, keys, blocks)
- The Counting Jar recording chart
- Index cards or 4-by-6-inch paper: at least 1 per student
- Paper plates: 1 per student
- Collections of countable objects

Calendar

What Happens

Together the group reads a story about keeping track of the days until someone's birthday. Students then explore the classroom calendar, which will be used in an ongoing classroom routine. Their work focuses on:

■ developing a sense of time (days, weeks)

■ viewing the calendar as a tool for keeping track of time and events

■ counting on the calendar

■ connecting number names, numerals, and quantities

Materials and Preparation

■ Obtain a copy of *Only Six More Days* by Marisabina Russo (Puffin Books, 1988), in big book form if possible.

■ Prepare a classroom calendar, with pockets or removable numbers, for the current month. Use cards or tags for special days, such as days off from school, trips, visitors, or birthdays. You might add a picture that will help students recognize each special event (for example, a cupcake with a candle, or a picture of the zoo).

■ Hang the calendar where students can easily see it when they are gathered as a whole group. Place all the cards (month, days of the week, numerals, and the "today" and special day tags) in the appropriate spaces. All cards should be visible (face up) so that students can see the days for the entire month.

■ Use a window or marker to indicate which day is today. You might make a movable border or frame to surround the number, or use a transparent colored square over the date.

■ Have several other examples of calendars to show to the class.

Draw attention to the classroom calendar and ask students about its purpose.

Who has an idea about what a calendar is? Where do you see calendars? What do people use them for? Have you even seen or used a calendar, or seen someone else use one?

Show several other kinds of calendars as well, to give students a wider variety of types to relate to and to expand their idea of what a calendar is. Some students will have some notion of what a calendar is and what we use it for, while others will have had little experience with them.

After students have shared their ideas, introduce the book *Only Six More Days* by Marisabina Russo.

Note: This story is about a little boy who is anxiously awaiting his birthday and uses a calendar to keep track of how many more days he has to wait. Some cultural and religious groups de-emphasize or do not celebrate individual birthdays. If your school has a policy precluding talk about birthdays or birthday celebrations, or if this story won't make sense given the make-up of your class, you might tell your own story about waiting for an upcoming special event in your classroom—perhaps a special visitor is coming, or there's a vacation day, or a school-wide concert or other program. If you use the birthday story, keep discussion open so that students can share the customs in their families.

As I read this book, think about how the characters in the story use calendars and why they use them. You can also look at the illustrations to see if there are any calendars in the pictures.

As you read this story, or after you have finished reading it, briefly discuss those questions with students.

Who in this story used a calendar? Why did he or she need a calendar? What did he or she use it for? How did he or she use a calendar?

See the **Dialogue Box**, Only Six More Days **(p. 47)**. for one class's discussion of this story as they read it.

Our Calendar

Gather students around the classroom calendar. All the numbers (dates) for the month should be in place and visible. Also, any special-day markers should have been placed on the correct dates.

Spend about 10 or 15 minutes introducing the calendar and the calendar routine you will revisit, possibly daily, throughout the year. For information on why this activity was chosen as a routine for kindergarten, and how students' mathematical work with it will progress over this year, see the discussion of Calendar in the section About Classroom Routines (p. 70).

This is a calendar that we are going to use all year, to keep track of time and special events. It shows us that the name of this month is September. What do you notice about our calendar for September?

Students will notice a wide variety of things, from the colors of different parts of the calendar, to the numbers and letters, to the tags for today and other special days. If students do not comment on any of these features, you will want to briefly mention and discuss them. Depending on your students' attention and the amount of time you have, you might discuss each feature today, or you might focus on some features the first time you investigate the calendar, and other features when you revisit the calendar at a later date.

The **Dialogue Box**, What's a Calendar? (p. 51), demonstrates what one group of kindergarten students observed about their classroom calendar.

Alexa noticed that our calendar had letters on it. Where do you see letters on our calendar?

Encourage students to find words on the calendar. Briefly explain what the words are and what they mean.

This big word up here tells us the name of the *month*. This month is September. These other words down here are *the days of the week*—Monday, Tuesday, Wednesday, Thursday, Friday, Saturday, and Sunday.

Take some time to discuss the numbers on the calendar and what they mean.

Felipe noticed that our calendar had numbers on it. Who has an idea about what those numbers mean?

Some students will have an idea about what the numbers on the calendar are for, while others will have a hard time recognizing many or any of the numerals.

The numbers on our calendar are for keeping track of the days in a month. So the number 1 *[point to it]* was the first day of September, and the number 2 was the second day of September. How many days do you think there are in the whole month of September?

Encourage students to share and explain their ideas, and then count the numbers on your calendar together as a group. Encourage students to count together with you. As happens when you are counting the students for attendance, you may find that the group can count aloud together much farther than many individual students in your class could count alone. Continue all through the month to 30, even as students drop out of the count. Remember that students learn how to count by having many opportunities to count and to see and hear others count.

Point out the special marker that shows "Today," and explain that this is how they can always tell on the classroom calendar which day is today.

Just like Ben, the little boy in the story we read, we are going to use our calendar to keep track of time and of special events. Each day we will put the Today tag on the day that is today. Today is the [18th] of September, so I'm going to put the Today tag on the number [18].

If you have students who know the counting sequence that far, ask them to count individually to the number that represents today. You can also do so together as a class.

Finally, review with students the other special events you've placed on the calendar, talking about what they represent and when they will happen.

Several of you noticed that there were some special cards on our calendar. Let's take a closer look at those special tags. What do you think they mean?

Encourage students to make predictions about those days based on how the cards are illustrated or labeled.

For more discussion on using the calendar daily in class, see About Classroom Routines: Calendar (p. 70).

When you introduce students to the Calendar routine, consider the questions below. As your students become more familiar with this routine and with the monthly calendar, and as you introduce some of the variations suggested in the full description of this routine (p. 70), adjust your observations to reflect the new activities.

- What do students know about calendars? What do they notice about the calendar for September? What information do they attend to? the letters or words? numerals? tags for special days? colors?
- Do students know the names of the days of the week? Can they identify "today" on the calendar?
- How comfortable are students with counting on the calendar? Do they know the sequence of number names? Do they forget or mix the order of some of the numbers? Which ones?

Focus Time Follow-Up

Choice Time

Following this Focus Time introduction of the Calendar routine, students explore a new material, interlocking cubes, during Choice Time. They also revisit the Counting Jar, introduced in the previous investigation, after you change the materials or the number of items inside the jar. In addition, choose any of the classroom materials already introduced (color tiles, pattern blocks, Geoblocks) or other materials you would like to introduce, for students to continue exploring during Choice Time. Consider rotating these materials every few days.

Exploring Interlocking Cubes

Counting Jar

Exploring Materials (Teacher's Choice)

Only Six More Days

The teacher prepares to read the class a story as an introduction to keeping track of time and events on the calendar.

We're going to be reading this book. The title of the book is *Only Six More Days*, **and it was written by Marisabina Russo. Take a look at the cover. What do you notice?**

Gabriela: There are lots of colors.

Luke: I think it's about a birthday.

Why do you think a birthday?

Kylie: There are cards.

Ravi: And hats.

Tess: That's a birthday cake.

And even this says "party" *[points to one of the invitations on the cover]*—**do you know what it's called? An invitation. Who do you think is having the party?** *[A few students think the little boy is.]* **Why do you think so?**

Renata: Because he's in the picture.

But there's a girl, too.

Kylie: I think the boy is having the birthday because he's making the cards.

After reading the first page, the teacher asks students what they notice.

Renata: The sister is being bad to him.

Ravi: She wasn't nice to Sam.

Brendan: She's not very polite.

Gabriela: The girl's not paying attention to birthdays.

Kylie: She is kind of rude.

Luke: She doesn't look happy.

Ben looks really happy. What is he looking at?

Tess: His birthday.

What do you mean, his birthday? What's he pointing at?

Brendan: A calendar.

Can you tell what month? I'll give you a hint: It rains a lot during this month.

Luke: Summer?

Summer is a season during the year. This month is not in the summer.

Gabriela: It's April.

Renata: My birthday's in April.

And can you tell what number he's pointing to?

Xing-Qi: It's 9.

As they continue to read, the teacher asks students why the girl seems so unhappy.

Luke: Because it's not her birthday.

Gabriela: Everyone is paying more attention to Ben's birthday than hers.

Tess: She's mad it's closer to his birthday, not hers. *[The teacher uses this opportunity to introduce the word* jealous.*]*

After reading "Hooray, hooray, I'm five today! I'll never be four again!" the teacher takes a quick survey of the ages of students.

How many kids in our class are 5 years old? *[Show of hands.]* **How many are 4?** *[Show of hands.]* **How many are 6?** *[Show of hands.]*

They continue reading, pausing at the page where the mother talks with the sister about her birthday.

What do you think the Mom showed her?

Kylie: Her birthday. It's next.

Oscar: She showed her the calendar where her birthday is.

Tess: My mom keeps our birthdays on the calendar, too. Mine is in November, right after Halloween.

Yes, keeping track of birthdays is one way that people use a calendar.

Choice Time

Exploring Interlocking Cubes

What Happens

Students freely explore interlocking cubes, a material that's useful for activities in pattern and counting, as well as for making three-dimensional constructions. Their work focuses on:

- exploring interlocking cubes and their attributes
- establishing routines for using and caring for interlocking cubes

Materials and Preparation

- Divide the class set of interlocking cubes into smaller bins or shoe boxes for use at more than one station. Include small cups, yogurt containers, or cans to use as scoops (optional).

Activity

Introduce the interlocking cubes to students in the same way that you have introduced other new materials. Explain where they can be found in the classroom and how they are to be used and cared for.

Point out that these cubes can be snapped together on every side. This is one of the most important features of this material, because it allows students to build three-dimensional constructions. Quickly demonstrate how the cubes can be snapped together in many different directions.

We'll be using these cubes a lot in our mathematics this year. We have already used them to build an attendance stick. How else do you think we might use them?

Interlocking cubes are an especially popular material in kindergarten, but they also present some unique management issues. After an initial talk with students about where the cubes can be found and how they are to be stored, you may want to revisit this topic after a few days of use, to discuss any issues that have arisen. If there are problems with sharing, role-playing can help students find a comfortable solution. Continue to reassure students about the availability of these materials to them over time.

Interlocking cubes lend themselves to making interesting and complicated 3-D structures and models—including guns and other weapons. If this issue presents itself, you may want to formulate class rules about making toy weapons.

Observing the Students

Observe students while they freely explore the interlocking cubes.

- How do students use the cubes? Do they stack them or use them to make long rods? Do they construct things that capitalize on the interlocking feature? Do they lay them flat to make designs or pictures? How do they describe the cubes and their creations?

- What do students create with the cubes? Do they label their constructions as representing familiar objects (this is a TV; this is a tall building)?

- Do any students try to copy each others' constructions? If so, how easy or hard is this task for them?

Sharing Our Work Plan a few times for students to share some of the work they have been doing with the interlocking cubes.

What do you like about using the cubes? How are they the same as or different from the Geoblocks? the color tiles?

Students often want to save their constructions made from cubes. Depending on the size of your class and the amount of cubes that you have, you may want to establish a "saving policy." Some groups have together decided on such a policy, quite often proposing that things can be saved for as much as a week. However, the students very quickly vote to alter that policy when they realize that after only a few days, there are very few cubes left to use during Choice Time. For many classrooms, saving constructions until the end of the day seems to satisfy the need to save a project for a period of time, and often allows enough time for constructions to be shared with peers or family members.

Variation

When students seem ready to do more directed work with the cubes, ask them to build something using a limited amount of cubes, such as 15. Notice how they count the cubes. Are they accurate? Do they have a way of keeping track of which cubes they have and have not counted? Do students have a grasp of one-to-one correspondence, saying only one number for one cube?

Encouraging Students to Think, Reason, and Share Ideas

Students need to take an active role in mathematics class. They must do more than get correct answers; they must think critically about their ideas, give reasons for their answers, and communicate their ideas to others. Reflecting on one's thinking and learning is a challenge for all learners, but even the youngest students can begin to engage in this important aspect of mathematics learning.

Teachers can help students develop their thinking and reasoning. By asking "How did you find your answer?" or "How do you know?" you encourage students to explain their thinking. If these questions evoke answers such as "I just knew it" or no response at all, you might reflect back something you observed as they were working, such as, "I noticed that you made two towers of cubes when you were solving this problem." This gives students a concrete example they can use in thinking about and explaining how they found their solutions.

You can also encourage students to record their ideas by building concrete models, drawing pictures, or starting to print numbers and words. Just as we encourage students to draw pictures that tell stories before they are fluent readers and writers, we should help them see that their mathematical ideas can be recorded on paper. When students are called on to share this work with the class, they learn that their mathematical thinking is valued and they develop confidence in their ideas. Because communicating about ideas is central to learning mathematics, it is important to establish the expectation that students will describe their work and their thinking, even in kindergarten.

There is a delicate balance between the value of having students share their thinking and the ability of 5- and 6-year-olds to sit and listen for extended periods of time. In kindergarten classes where we observed the best discussions, talking about mathematical ideas and sharing work from a math activity were as much a part of the classroom culture as sitting together to listen to a story, to talk about a new activity, or to anticiapte an upcoming event.

Early in the school year, whole-class discussions are best kept short and focused. For example, after exploring pattern blocks, students might simply share experiences with the new material in a discussion structured almost as list-making:

What did you notice about pattern blocks? Who can tell us something different?

With questions like these, lots of students can participate without one student taking a lot of time.

Later in the year, when students are sharing their strategies for solving problems, you can use questions that allow many students to participate at once by raising their hands. For example:

Luke just shared that he solved the problem by counting out one cube for every person in our classroom. Who else solved the problem the same way Luke did?

In this way, you acknowledge the work of many students without everyone sharing individually.

Sometimes all students should have a chance to share their math work. You might set up a special "sharing shelf" or display area to set out or post student work. By gathering the class around the shelf or display, you can easily discuss the work of every student.

The ability to reflect on one's own thinking and to consider the ideas of others evolves over time, but even young students can begin to understand that an important part of doing mathematics is being able to explain your ideas and give reasons for your answers. In the process, they see that there can be many ways of finding solutions to the same problem. Over the year, your students will become more comfortable thinking about their solution methods, explaining them to others, and listening to their classmates explain theirs.

What's a Calendar?

The following discussion took place in a kindergarten class early in the school year during the daily morning meeting. The monthly calendar in this class was a rectangular board with metal cup hooks arranged in rows of seven. The date cards for the month of September hung on the board, numbered 1 to 30, some with tags noting special events. Next to this monthly calendar there hung a wall calendar opened to the month of September. This teacher started by finding out what the students already knew about calendars and how they are used.

This morning we are going to begin our meeting by talking about our classroom calendar. I was wondering, does anyone know what a calendar is for, or what a calendar shows?

Jacob: It helps you keep track.

Shanique: It's so you don't forget to do something. My dad is always forgetting to do something.

Thomas: Well, mine at home has pages that you rip off it.

Miyuki: There are different kinds, like the kind that has a window on it.

Carlo: It lets you know the day and the months.

Shanique: It's so you don't forget your birthday.

Maddy: I would *never* forget my birthday. Umm, it's June 12. I think.

Renata: When you get to the end of a page, you tear it off, and the next one and the next one. It goes and goes.

You know a lot of things about calendars. Take a look at our classroom calendar. What to you notice about it?

Ayesha: It has cards with numbers on it.

Tarik: It's blue.

Miyuki: Some of the cards are yellow and some are green.

Yes, the green cards are the weekend days, Saturday and Sunday. The yellow cards are the days we usually come to school. These little tags, up here, tell the names of the days in the week.

Jacob: Like Wednesday is today. It has that thing around it.

This is the way that we will show what day it is on the calendar, by hanging this TODAY tag on the hook. Today is Wednesday.

Shanique: And today is 13. My brother is 13.

Some of you noticed that the calendar has cards with numbers on them. The numbers are for the days in the month. September has 30 days in it. So far, 13 of the days have gone by. Let's count them.

Henry: That day has a tag on it.

Justine: That's my birthday! It's tomorrow.

Kadim: And there's another birthday there. Hey! It goes *no birthday*, birthday, *no birthday,* birthday, *no birthday, no birthday, no birthday* . . . Oh. I thought it would go back and forth.

The teacher continues the discussion, explaining about the special tags on the calendar and what they mean. She was interested in Kadim's observation about the birthdays and makes a special note to ask the students if they notice any patterns on the calendar at tomorrow's meeting.

Today's Question

Focus Time

Today's Question (p. 54)

Students use their name cards or name pins to register their response to a survey question with two possible answers: Are you a girl or a boy? This activity, Today's Question, involves the class in collecting, representing, and discussing data. Today's Question is another classroom routine suggested for use throughout the kindergarten year.

Choice Time

Continuing from Investigation 3

Counting Jar (p. 32)

Exploring Materials (Teacher's Choice)

Mathematical Emphasis

- Collecting and recording data
- Counting and comparing the number of students in two different groups
- Exploring materials that will be used in this unit and throughout the curriculum

Teacher Support

Dialogue Box

What Do You Notice? (p. 60)

What to Plan Ahead of Time

Focus Time Materials

Today's Question

- Name cards or name pins (as prepared in Investigation 1 for the Attendance routine)
- Chart paper or tagboard, a sheet about 12 by 36 inches, prepared as a survey chart with *Today's Question* at the top, followed by the question "Are you a girl or a boy?" and two columns below, headed *Girl* and *Boy,* with a simple sketch as a visual cue (see p. 72 for chart illustration)
- Attendance stick (from Investigation 1)

Choice Time Materials

Counting Jar

- Counting Jar with 5–12 countable items (cubes, balls, keys, blocks)
- Counting Jar recording sheet prepared in Investigation 3
- Index cards or 4-by-6-inch paper: at least 1 per student
- Paper plates: 1 per student
- Collections of countable objects

Exploring Materials (Teacher's Choice)

- Class sets of pattern blocks, interlocking cubes, color tiles, Geoblocks, or other materials, with scoops as needed
- Unlined paper and coloring materials, available

Today's Question

What Happens

Students are introduced to Today's Question, a data activity they will revisit throughout the year. In this first survey, they collect data abut the number of boys and the number of girls in their classroom. They count the number of students in each category and then count the total number of responses on the graph. Their work focuses on:

- collecting data that fall into two groups
- counting and comparing the number of students in different groups
- establishing one-to-one correspondence between a group and the data collected

Materials and Preparation

- Arrange students' name cards on a table where everyone can see and reach them, or make available their name pins.
- Post the prepared survey chart for Today's Question, "Are you a girl or a boy?" within reach of every student.

Activity

Are You a Girl or a Boy?

The first step of Today's Question is simply collecting students' responses, or the *data*. You might do this in one of two ways. If you have been using name pins with the Attendance routine, students can simply clip their pins to the side of the chart in the appropriate column. Alternatively, students can print their names on the chart, using their name cards as a reference.

If you plan to work with the data during a morning whole-group meeting, you might have students find their name cards or name pins and record their responses as they come into your classroom first thing in the morning. If the activity is scheduled for later in the day, simply set aside a few minutes beforehand to explain the task and to give students the necessary time to find their name cards or pins and respond to the question on the chart.

In any case, plan to be available to read aloud the question on the chart, to help as needed with locating name cards or name pins, and to explain how students are to record their responses on the chart.

Before gathering students to discuss the data, check to see which name cards or name pins remain unused. Some will belong to students who are absent; the rest indicate students who have not yet done this preparatory activity. Remind the class that everyone needs to answer Today's Question. Don't add the names of any absent students to the chart at this time; students will place them in the proper column during a subsequent activity.

If using name cards, collect them after students have signed in and store them for continued use in the Attendance routine and with other rounds of Today's Question.

Activity

Looking at Our Data

Refer the group to today's attendance figures to establish the number of students in class. Then direct attention to the survey chart for Today's Question.

Everyone answered a question today, and you used this chart to do it. Who can tell us about what you did?

If you are a girl, you placed your name in this column. If you are a boy, you placed your name in this other column. Take a minute to look carefully at our chart. What are some things you notice?

Students will likely notice a wide range of things about the chart and the data they have recorded on it. The **Dialogue Box,** What Do You Notice? (p. 60), offers some typical observations made by kindergartners.

Some students might make observations about the graph that have little or nothing to do with the data, such as, "I notice that the paper is white," or "Some kids' names have S's and some do not." Accept these observations as you would accept any others. Students will learn more about looking at data over time by having repeated opportunities to hear each other comment on data that they have collected.

What does this chart tell us about the people in our class?

If students do not count or suggest counting the number of boys and the number of girls, do so now.

I'm interested in finding out how many girls and how many boys there are in our classroom today. Who has an idea about how we could find that out?

Students might suggest counting the names on the lists while others will suggest counting the girls and boys in the class. Try the ideas that students suggest. Having several children count reinforces the idea that double-checking is an important strategy in counting accurately.

Keep in mind, however, that when more than one child counts, they often arrive at differing totals. Some students will forget to count themselves; others will not say one number name for each child; and still others may skip numbers in the sequence or skip children in the circle. Many students will not be concerned about totals that differ. Call their attention to such discrepancies and encourage students to consider possible reasons for getting different answers. Be sure to focus such discussions on strategies for counting and keeping track of a group of people, without placing any emphasis on who counted correctly.

Once students have determined the number of girls and boys in the class by counting both the actual children and the names in each column of the chart, draw their attention to the fact that the two counts were the same.

Hmm. When we counted the number of girls in our class, and we counted the number of names on the "Girl" side of the chart, we got the same number. Does anyone have an idea why that happened?

After gathering responses, ask students to think about the group of boys in the same way. Then focus on the total number of names on the chart as compared to the total number of students in the meeting area.

At the beginning of our group meeting, we figured out that there were [22] students in school today. I wonder how many names there are on this chart if we counted all of them?

After students share their ideas, count the names on the chart together as a group and then ask students to reflect on this information.

There are [22] names on the chart and there are [22] students in school today. Does it surprise you that those two numbers are the same?

Listen for explanations that suggest students may be making a one-to-one correspondence between the number of students in the class and the number of names on the chart. Some students may recognize that these should be the same number, however, many may not yet make this connection.

As you introduce this activity and when you repeat Today's Question at other times throughout the year, consider the following as you listen to and observe how students describe and discuss the data they have collected.

■ Do students seem to understand what the data represent? Can they describe in their own words what information is being collected?

■ What features of the representation do students notice? Do they comment on relevant features of the representation and the data? (For example, "There are more boys than girls," or "There are 12 girls on the graph.")

■ Are students able to make comparisons between the two groups? If the two groups are not equal, can they figure out which group has more? How do they do this? Do they compare the number of responses in each group?

■ Do students recognize that there is a one-to-one correspondence between the number of responses on the graph and the number of students present in class?

When you have established and discussed the number of names on the chart and the number of students in class today, call attention to the name cards or name pins of students who are absent. Read the names of those students and ask the class to decide which column they belong in.

Not everyone in our class is here today. Justine, Henry, and Ravi are absent today—one girl and two boys. We counted and found out that there are 12 girls in our class today, but we didn't count Justine. How many girls are there in our class when everyone is here? What about the boys?

After adding the names of absent students to the chart, count the total number of names on the chart with the group. Help students relate this information to the class attendance stick.

Adding Absent Students

We counted the names of all the boys in our class and all the girls in our class, and we found that there were 25 students in all. Let's take a look at the attendance stick. Who remembers how many cubes are in our stick? Let's count them to make sure they are all there.

Encourage students to count as you point to each cube, beginning with the cube numbered 1.

Today's Question is an activity, or routine, that we will do from time to time all year long. We call it "Today's" Question because each time we do it, there will be a different question of the day. Each time, we'll find out something else about the people in our class.

As you plan future sessions for this routine, think about choosing questions that are appropriate for your students. Consider what questions might raise sensitive issues. Also determine whether a question really has only two possible responses, or if you want to allow for a third column. Some teachers choose questions that involve students in making decisions about the classroom, or that help them plan for a new curriculum topic. Refer to the discussion of Today's Question in the section About Classroom Routines (p. 72) for more about these and other things to consider when choosing survey questions.

Focus Time Follow-Up

Choice Time

Following this Focus Time, students revisit the Counting Jar with yet another change of material or number of items. They also continue to explore the mathematical materials they will use throughout the year. Choose two or three of materials introduced earlier (pattern blocks, Geoblocks, color tiles, or interlocking cubes). Consider rotating these materials every few days. If students seem ready, consider some of the variations listed for these activities, such as recording designs on paper that reflect their constructions with color tiles (p. 13) or pattern blocks (p. 15), or the specified use of 15 interlocking cubes (p. 49).

Counting Jar

Exploring Materials (Teacher's Choice)

What Do You Notice?

When you are looking at data that the class has collected, asking students to explain what a particular survey or graph is about encourages them to interpret the information they have collected. All too often, students lose sight of the content and meaning of a data collection experience and simply focus on the process of collecting data. In this classroom, the students are making observations about the chart that represents the data for Today's Question: Are you a girl or a boy?

Let's look at the chart where everyone recorded an answer to the question, "Are you a girl or a boy?" If you are a girl, you wrote your name in this column. If you are a boy, you wrote your name in this other column. Take a minute to look carefully at our chart. What are some of the things you notice?

Luke: There's lots of names on it.

Carlo: The writing is in black and blue.

Renata: This one here is my name. *[She gets up and points to her name.]*

Kylie: And this one is my name: K-Y-L-I-E. Kylie. *[She also gets up and points to her name.]*

At this point, anticipating a trend, the teacher quickly has all the students acknowledge their names on the chart.

I want everyone to look very carefully at the chart. Using only your eyes, try to find your name. When you see it raise your hand. *[The teacher waits until most everyone's hand is raised, and then helps the two students who cannot find their names.]* **There are lots of names on this chart—in fact, everyone who is here today has their name on this chart. Are there other things you notice about the chart?**

Charlotte: There's more girls than boys.

Henry: There's lots of letters.

Tarik: This word *[points]* says *boys.* I'm in that group.

Thomas: And this word says *girls,* and I'm *not* in that group. *[He whispers, "Do you like girls?" to the boy next to him.]*

Charlotte said that there are more girls than boys. How can you tell that information?

Charlotte: The girls' line is longer. See, it goes down lower.

Felipe: You look at the two sides, and the girls have more on their side because it's got more names on it.

Henry: There is more of the space filled in on the girls' side. You can see it.

So you are comparing the girls' side to the boys' side, and the girls' side has more.

Ayesha: I know a different way. You can count. There's 1, 2, 3 *[continues up to]* 12 girls. There's 1, 2, 3 *[continues up to]* 10 boys. And 12 is more than 10.

So another way of figuring out which has more is to count and compare the numbers.

By asking students to make observations about the data they collected, this teacher was able to get a sense from the students what aspects of the chart were interesting to them. Although some students made observations about the graph that had little or nothing to do with the data, they were nonetheless accurate observations. From previous experience, this teacher knows that students will learn more about looking at data over time by having repeated opportunities to hear each other comment on data that they have collected.

About Color Tiles

Color tiles are one-inch square tiles that come in four colors: red, yellow, blue, and green. When young students use color tiles in their free play, they often stack them on top of each other to make tall towers, arrange them in long, flat snakes that travel across a table or along the classroom floor, or lay them flat to cover a specified area. They almost always discover that by standing them on one edge, close together in a line, they can be toppled over in sequence (like dominoes), much to the delight of the builder and all who are watching.

In the kindergarten *Investigations* curriculum, color tiles are used to investigate experiences in pattern, counting, and other number-related activities. For the unit *Pattern Trains and Hopscotch Paths,* students use tiles to copy, create, and extend and predict pattern sequences. In the unit *Collecting, Counting, and Measuring,* they grab and count handfuls of tiles and use them to investigate arrangements of 6.

Color tiles can be stored in the plastic buckets they come in. One bucket of 400 is generally enough for 8–10 students. If materials are limited, some teachers use a small container or measuring cup as a scoop to establish the amount of tiles students can use. For some activities, tiles will need to be separated into single-color bins. Students can help sort them. Shoe boxes or pie tins make convenient storage bins.

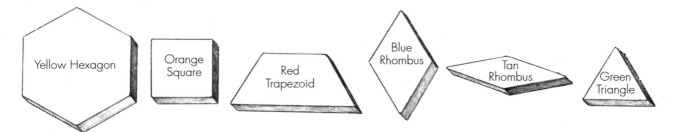

The pattern block set is made up of six geometric shapes in six colors.

- *Yellow hexagon.* A hexagon is a six-sided polygon. This block is a regular hexagon because all the sides and angles are equal.
- *Red trapezoid.* A trapezoid is a four-sided polygon that has one pair of parallel sides.
- *Green triangle.* A triangle is a three-sided polygon. This triangle is an equilateral triangle because all the sides and angles are equal.
- *Orange square.* A square is a four-sided polygon with four equal sides and angles. (A square is also a rectangle.)
- *Blue rhombus and tan rhombus.* These two shapes are both parallelograms—four-sided polygons with two pairs of parallel sides. They are a special kind of parallelogram, called a *rhombus*, that has four equal sides. (You might notice that the orange square is also a parallelogram with four equal sides, so it is actually a rhombus, too.)

Young children typically refer to the blue and tan blocks as *diamonds*. There is no need to discourage student use of this familiar term. As long as they are communicating effectively, let them use the language they are comfortable with while you continue to model use of the mathematical term *rhombus*.

The pattern blocks are related in a variety of ways. The length of every side is equal, except for the long side of the trapezoid, which is twice as long. The area of the blocks is also related. Two red trapezoids, three blue rhombuses, and six green triangles all have the same area as a yellow hexagon and can be arranged into a shape that is congruent with the yellow hexagon.

Thus, a red trapezoid is half a hexagon; a blue rhombus is one-third of a hexagon, and a green triangle is one-sixth.

Pattern blocks come in plastic bins for convenient classroom storage. If sharing is an issue, use smaller tubs or shoe boxes to split each set into smaller sets. The original set provides enough blocks for four to six students. You can limit the total number of blocks students may use by providing either a scoop for portioning out materials or a mat on which to work, thus limiting the amount of space they can cover.

Pattern blocks are used in the *Investigations* curriculum at every grade level. In kindergarten, pattern blocks are first introduced in the unit *Mathematical Thinking in Kindergarten,* and students use them to create and extend patterns in the unit *Pattern Trains and Hopscotch Paths.* In the data unit, *Counting Ourselves and Others,* students grab handfuls of these blocks and find a way to represent what they grabbed on paper. In the geometry unit, *Making Shapes and Building Blocks,* students use pattern blocks to fill in puzzle outlines. They also explore many ways to "make" the hexagon as they play a game called Fill the Hexagons. The *Shapes* software used with the geometry unit also has activities with pattern block shapes.

About Geoblocks

Geoblocks are a special set of three-dimensional wooden blocks. While similar to other kindergarten blocks (wooden unit blocks), they are smaller and are designed so that the blocks are related by volume. We live in a three-dimensional world, yet most of the geometry students do in school is concerned with two-dimensional shapes. We frequently use two-dimensional drawings to help us picture and represent three-dimensional things. For example, a blueprint provides instructions for building a house; a paper pattern, for cutting out and sewing a shirt; a diagram, for assembling a bike. One reason we include Geoblocks in the kindergarten materials is that it's important for students to work with three-dimensional materials and see the relationship between three- and two-dimensional shapes.

In the *Investigations* curriculum, students use Geoblocks in kindergarten and in the first and second grades. After the blocks are introduced in *Mathematical Thinking in Kindergarten,* they are formally used only in the geometry unit, *Making Shapes and Building Blocks.* However, we recommend that you make the Geoblocks available to students throughout the year, perhaps in a building area or during times such as indoor recess or free Choice Time. Most kindergartners love to build with these blocks; they build towers, towns, roads, ramps, bridges, and many other things. During this informal building time, they intuitively learn many of the characteristics of the blocks.

Because there are a limited number of Geoblocks, especially some types, sharing is often an issue. While there are lots of the smallest cubes (128), there are only two each of the largest blocks, and only four or six of many of the triangular blocks. To help with sharing, begin by separating each set of 330 Geoblocks into two equal sets, each set being enough for four or five students. Probably the easiest way to divide the main set of blocks is to find two identical blocks and put one in each set. Parent volunteers, aides, or older student volunteers can do this, although the sorting task is a good way for you to become familiar with the shapes yourself.

Encourage students to use only the blocks in their particular set. Before sending students off to explore and build, you might model ways of sharing and ways to request blocks (and to respond to requests). Students need to be able to accept the fact that the block they want may be important in someone else's construction, too. In some situations you might encourage students to combine buildings or to build together. Finally, students who cannot find a block they want can be encouraged or challenged to find two (or more) other blocks that combine to make the original. This is a possibility for most blocks in this set, which is one of their useful mathematical attributes.

Continued on next page

For your own information, there are five kinds of shapes in the Geoblock set. Before reading these descriptions, we suggest that you do your own sorting of the blocks, since they are probably less familiar to you than some of the other kindergarten materials. Once you have sorted the blocks into groups that you think "go together," the descriptions will probably make more sense. Kindergarten students are not expected to learn the formal names or descriptions of Geoblock shapes.

All the shapes are *polyhedra,* three-dimensional solid shapes with flat faces. These are the five general categories:

Rectangular prisms. Prisms have two opposite faces that are the same size and shape (congruent). All other faces, connecting these two opposite faces, are rectangles. In *rectangular prisms,* the two opposite faces are rectangles, so all six faces are rectangles. Most boxes are rectangular prisms. You can also call these shapes *rectangular solids.*

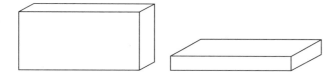

Rectangular prisms

Square prisms. These are a special kind of rectangular prism. They have two opposite faces that are congruent squares. The other four faces are rectangles.

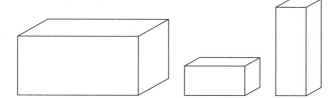

Square prisms

Cubes. Just as the square is a special kind of rectangle, the cube is a special kind of rectangular prism in which all the faces are squares.

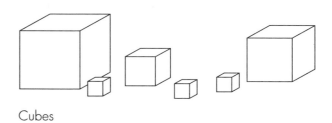

Cubes

Triangular prisms. These prisms have two opposite faces that are congruent triangles. As in any prism, the faces that connect this pair are all rectangles.

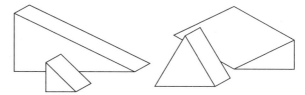

Triangular prisms

Pyramid. There is one kind of pyramid in the Geoblock set. Pyramids look different from prisms. They have one base, which can be any polygon. The rest of the faces are triangles that meet in a single point (vertex). The pyramid in the Geoblock collection is a *square pyramid.* It has a square base and four triangular faces.

Pyramid

Attendance

Taking the daily attendance and talking about who is and who is not in school are familiar activities in many kindergarten classrooms. Through the Attendance routine, students get repeated practice in counting a quantity that is significant to them: the number of people in their class. This is real data that they see, work with, and relate to every day. As they count the boys and girls in their class or the cubes in the attendance stick, they are counting quantities into the 20s. They begin to see the need to develop strategies for counting, including ways to double-check and to organize or keep track of a count.

Counting is an important mathematical idea in the kindergarten curriculum. As students count, they are learning how our number system is constructed, and they are building the knowledge they need to begin to solve numerical problems. They are also developing critical understandings about how numbers are related to each other and how the counting sequence is related to the quantities they are counting.

In *Investigations,* students are introduced to the Attendance routine during the first unit of the kindergarten sequence, *Mathematical Thinking in Kindergarten.* The basic activity is described here, followed by suggested variations for daily use throughout the school year.

The Attendance routine, with its many variations, is a powerful activity for 5- and 6-year-olds and one they never seem to tire of, perhaps because it deals with a topic that is of high interest: themselves and their classmates!

Materials and Preparation

The Attendance routine involves an attendance stick and name cards or "name pins" to be used with a display board. (Many teachers begin the year with name cards and later substitute name pins as a tool for recording the data.)

To make the attendance stick you need interlocking cubes of a single color, one for each class member, and dot stickers to number the cubes.

To make name cards, print each student's first name on a small card (about 2 by 3 inches). Add a photo if possible. If you don't have school photos or camera and film, you might ask students to bring in small photos of themselves from home.

For "name pins," print each student's name on both sides of a clothespin, being sure the name is right side up whether the clip is to the right or to the left.

Name cards might be displayed in two rows on the floor or on a display board. The board should have "Here" and "Not Here" sections, each divided into as many rows or columns as there are students in your class. To display name cards on the board, you might use pockets, cup hooks, or small pieces of Velcro or magnetic tape. Name pins can be clipped down the sides of a sturdy vertical board.

Collecting Attendance Data

How Many Are We? With the whole group, establish the total number of students in the class this year by going around the circle and counting the number of children present.

Encourage students to count aloud with you. The power of the group can often get the class as a whole much further in the counting sequence than many individuals could actually count. While one or two children may be able to count to the total number of students in the class, do not be surprised or concerned if, by the end of your count, you are the lone voice. Students learn the counting sequence and how to count by having many opportunities to count, and to see and hear others counting.

When you have counted those present, acknowledge any absent students and add them to the total number in your class.

Counting Around the Circle Counting Around the Circle is a way to count and double-check the number of students in a group. Designate one person in the circle as the first person and begin counting off. That is, the first person says "1," the second person says "2," and so on around the circle. As students are learning how to count around the circle, you can help by pointing to the person whose turn it is to count. Some students will likely need help with identifying the next number in the counting sequence. Encouraging students to help each other figure out what number might come next establishes a climate of asking for and giving help to others.

Counting Around the Circle takes some time for students to grasp—both the procedure itself and its meaning. For some students, it will not be apparent that the number they say stands for the number of people who have counted thus far. A common response from kindergartners first learning to count off is to relate the number they say to a very familiar number, their age. Expect someone to say, for example, "I'm not 8, I'm 5!" Be prepared to explain that the purpose of counting off is to find out how many students are in the circle, and that the number 8 stands for the people who have been counted so far.

Representing Attendance Data

The Attendance Stick An attendance stick is a concrete model, made from interlocking cubes, that represents the total number of students in the classroom. For young students, part of knowing that there are 25 students in the class is seeing a representation of 25 students. The purpose of this classroom routine is not only to familiarize students with the counting sequence of numbers above 10, but also to help students relate these numbers to the quantities that they represent.

To make an attendance stick, distribute an interlocking cube to each student in the class. After counting the number of students present, turn their attention to the cubes.

We just figured out that there are [25] students in our classroom today. When you came to group meeting this morning, I gave everybody one cube. Suppose we collected all the cubes **and snapped them together. How many cubes do you think we would have?**

Collect each student's cube and snap them together into a vertical tower or stick. Encourage students to count with you as you add on cubes. Also add cubes for any absent students.

Ayesha is not here today. Right now our stick has 24 cubes in it because there are 24 students in school today. If we add Ayesha's cube, how many cubes will be in our stick?

Using small dot stickers, number the cubes. Display the attendance stick prominently in the group meeting area and refer to it each time you take attendance.

By counting around, we found that 22 of you are here today. Let's count up to 22 on the attendance stick. Count with me: 1, 2, 3 . . . *[when you reach 22, snap off the remaining cubes].* **So this is how many students are not here—who wants to count them?**

In this way, every day the class sees the attendance stick divided into two parts to represent the students HERE and NOT HERE.

Name Cards or Name Pins Name cards or pins are another concrete way to represent the students. Whereas the attendance stick represents *how many students* are in the class, name cards or pins provide additional data about *who* these people are.

Once students can recognize their name in print, they can simply select their card or pin from the class collection as they enter the classroom each day. At a group meeting, the names can be displayed to show who is here and who is not here, perhaps as a graph on the floor or on some type of display board.

Examining Attendance Data

Comparing Groups In addition to counting, the Attendance routine offers experience with part-whole relationships as students divide the total number into groups, such as PRESENT and ABSENT (HERE and NOT HERE) or GIRLS and BOYS. As they compare these groups, they are beginning to analyze the data and compare quantities: Which is more? Which is less? *How many* more or less? While the numbers for the groups can change on any given day, the sum of the two groups remains the same. Understanding part-whole relationships is a central part of both sound number sense and a facility with numbers.

The attendance stick and the name cards or name pins are useful tools for representing and comparing groups. One day you might use the attendance stick to count and compare how many students are present and absent; another day you might use name cards or pins the same way. Once students are familiar with the routine, you can represent the same data using more than one tool.

To compare groups, choose a day when everyone is in school. Count the number of boys and the number of girls.

Are there more boys than girls? How do you know? How many more?

Have the boys make a line and the girls make a line opposite them. Count the number of students in each line and compare the two lines.

Which has more? How many more?

Use the name cards or the attendance stick to double-check this information.

Once the total number of boys and girls is established, you can use this information to make daily comparisons.

Count the number of girls. Are all the girls HERE today? If not, how many are NOT HERE? How do you know? Can we show this information using the name cards? *[Repeat for the boys.]*

If we know that two girls and two boys are NOT HERE, how many in all are NOT HERE in school today? How do you know? Let's use the name cards to double-check.

When students are very familiar with this routine, with the total number in their class, and with making and comparing groups, you can

pose a more difficult problem. For example:

If we know four students are NOT HERE in school today, how many students are HERE today? What are all the ways we can figure that out, without counting off?

Some students might suggest breaking four cubes off the attendance stick and counting the rest. Others might suggest counting back from the total number of students. Still others might suggest counting up from 4 to the total number of students.

In addition to being real data that students can see and relate to every day, attendance offers manageable numbers to work with. Repetition of this routine over the school year is important; only after students are familiar with the routine will they begin to focus on the numbers involved. Gradually, they will start to make some important connections between counting and comparing quantities.

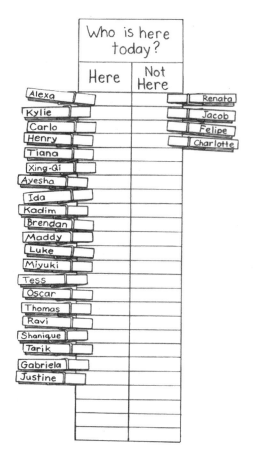

Counting Jar

Counting is the foundation for much of the number work that students do in kindergarten and in the primary grades. Children learn to count by counting and hearing others count. Similarly, they learn about quantity through repeated experiences with organizing and counting sets of objects. The Counting Jar routine offers practice with all of these.

When students count sets of objects in the jar, they are practicing the counting sequence. As in the Attendance routine, they begin to see the need to develop strategies for counting, including ways to double-check and keep track of what they have counted. By recording the number of objects they have counted, students gain experience in representing quantity and conveying mathematical information to others. Creating a new equivalent set gives them not only another opportunity to count, but also a chance to compare the two amounts.

Does my set have the same number as the set in the jar? How do I know?

The jar has 8 and I have 7. I need 1 more because 8 is 1 more than 7.

As students work, they are developing a real sense of both numbers and quantities.

The Counting Jar routine is introduced in the first unit of the kindergarten curriculum, *Mathematical Thinking in Kindergarten.* The basic activity is described here, followed by suggested variations for use throughout the school year on a weekly basis.

Materials and Preparation

Obtain a clear plastic container, at least 6 inches tall and 4–5 inches in diameter. Fill it with a number of interesting objects that are uniform in size and not too small, such as golf or table tennis balls, small blocks or tiles, plastic animals, or walnuts in the shell. The total should be a number that is manageable for most students in your class; initially, 5 to 12 objects would be appropriate quantities.

Prepare a recording sheet on chart paper. At the top, write *The Counting Jar,* followed by the name of the material inside. Along the bottom, write a number line. Some students might use this number line to help them count objects or as a reference for writing numerals. Place each number in a box to clearly distinguish one from another.

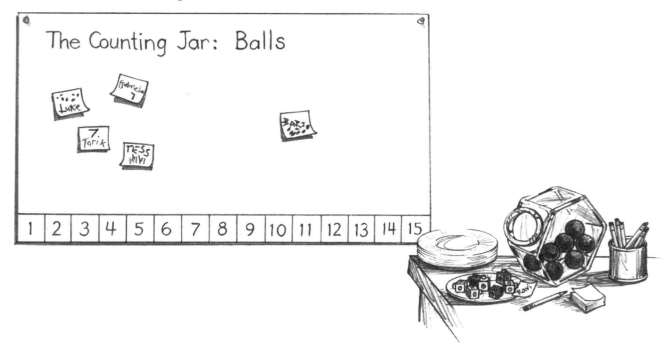

Laminate this chart so that students can record their counts on the chart with stick-on notes, write-on/wipe-off markers, or small scraps of paper and tape; these can later be removed and the chart reused.

Also make available one paper plate for each student and sets of countable materials, such as cubes, buttons, keys, teddy bear counters, or color tiles, so that students can create a new set of materials that corresponds to the quantity in the Counting Jar.

Counting

How Many in the Jar? This routine has three basic steps:

- Working individually or in pairs, students count the objects in the Counting Jar.

- Students make a representation that shows how many objects are in the jar and place their response on the chart.

- Students count out another set of objects equivalent to the quantity in the Counting Jar. They place this new set on a paper plate, write their name on the plate, and display their equivalent collection near the Counting Jar.

As you use the Counting Jar throughout the school year, call attention to it in a whole-group meeting whenever you have changed the material or the amount inside the jar. Then leave it in a convenient location for two or three days so that everyone has a chance to count. After most students have counted individually, meet with the whole class and count the contents together.

Note: Some kindergarten teachers use a very similar activity for estimation practice. We exclude the task of estimation from the basic activity because until students have a sense of quantity, a sense of how much 6 is, a sense of what 10 balls look like compared to 10 cubes, it is difficult for them to estimate or predict how large a quantity is. When students are more familiar with the routine and have begun to develop a sense of quantity, you might include the variations suggested for estimation.

One More, One Less When students can count the materials in the jar with a certain amount of accuracy and understanding, try this variation for work with the ideas "one more than" and "one less than." As you offer the Counting Jar activity, ask students to create a set of objects with one more (or less) than the amount in the jar.

Filling the Jar Ourselves When the Counting Jar routine is firmly established, give individuals or pairs of students the responsibility for filling the jar. Discuss with them an appropriate quantity to put in the jar or suggest a target number, and let students decide on suitable objects to put in the jar.

At-Home Counting Jars Suggest to families that they set up a Counting Jar at home. Offer suggestions for different materials and appropriate quantities. Family members can take turns putting sets of objects in the jar for others to count.

Estimation

Is It More Than 5? To introduce the idea of estimation, show students a set of five objects identical to those in the Counting Jar. This gives students a concrete amount for reference to base their estimate on. As they look at the known quantity, ask them to think about whether there are *more than* five objects in the jar. The number in the reference group can grow as the number of objects in the jar changes, and you can begin to ask "Is the amount in the jar more than 8? more than 10?"

More or Less Than Yesterday? You can also encourage students to develop estimation skills when the material in the jar stays the same over several days but the quantity changes. In this situation, students can use reasoning like this:

Last time, when there were 8 blocks in the jar, it was filled up to *here*. Now it's a little higher, so I think there are 10 or 11 blocks.

Calendar

"Calendar," with its many rituals and routines, is a familiar kindergarten activity. Perhaps the most important idea, particularly for young students, is viewing the calendar as a real-world tool that we use to keep track of time and events. As students work with the calendar, they become more familiar with the sequence of days, weeks, and months, and relationships among these periods of time. Time and the passage of time are challenging ideas for most 5- and 6-year-olds, and the ideas need to be linked to their own direct experiences. For example, explaining that an event will occur *after* a child's birthday or *before* a familiar holiday will help place that event in time for them.

The Calendar routine is introduced in the first unit of the kindergarten curriculum, *Mathematical Thinking in Kindergarten.* The basic activity is described here, followed by suggested variations for daily use throughout the school year.

Materials and Preparation

In most kindergarten classrooms, a monthly calendar is displayed where everyone can see it when the class gathers as a whole group. A calendar with date cards that can be removed or rearranged allows for greater flexibility than one without. Teachers make different choices about how to display numbers on this calendar. We recommend displaying all the days, from 1 to 30 or 31, all month long. This way the sequence of numbers and the total number of days are

always visible, thus giving students a sense of the month as a whole.

You can use stick-on labels to highlight special days such as birthdays, class trips or events, non-school days, or holidays. Similarly, find some way to identify *today* on the calendar. Some teachers have a special star or symbol to clip on today's date card, or a special tag, much like a picture frame, that hangs over today's date.

A Sense of Time

The Monthly Calendar When first introducing the calendar, ask students what they notice. They are likely to mention a wide variety of things, including the colors they see on the calendar, pictures, numbers, words, how the calendar is arranged, and any special events they know are in that particular month. If no one brings it up, ask students what calendars are for and how we use them.

At the beginning of each month, involve students in organizing the dates and recording special events on the calendar. The following questions help them understand the calendar as a tool for keeping track of events in time:

If our trip to the zoo is on the 13th, on which day should we hang the picture of a lion?

Is our trip tomorrow? the next day? this week?

What day of the week will we go to the zoo?

How Much Longer? Many students eagerly anticipate upcoming events or special days. Ask students to figure out how much longer it is until something, or how many days have passed since something happened. For example:

How many more days is it until Alexa's birthday?

Today is November 4. How many more days is it until November 10?

How many days until the end of the month?

How many days have gone by since our parent breakfast?

Ask students to share their strategies for finding the number of days. Initially many students will count each subsequent day. Later some students may begin to find answers by using their growing knowledge of calendar structure and number relationships:

> I knew there were three more days in this row, and I added them to the three in the next row. That's six more days.

Calculating "how many more days" on the calendar is not an easy task. Quite likely students will not agree on what days to count. Consider the following three good answers, all different, to this teacher's question:

Today is October 4. Ida's birthday is on October 8. How many more days until her birthday?

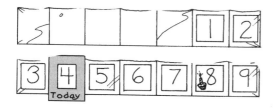

Tess: I think there are four more days because it's 4 . . . *[counting on her fingers]* 5, 6, 7, 8.

Ravi: There are three more days. See? *[He points to the three calendar dates between October 4 and October 8—5, 6, and 7—and counts three date cards.]*

Gabriela: It's five more days until her birthday. *[Using the calendar, she points to today and counts "1, 2, 3, 4 , 5," ending on October 8.]*

All of these students made sense of their answers and, considering their reasoning, all three were correct. That's why, when asking "how many more?" questions based on the calendar, it is important also to ask students to explain their thinking.

Numbers on the Calendar

Counting Days The calendar is a place where students can daily visit and become more familiar with the sequence of counting numbers up to 31. Because the numbers on the calendar represent the number of days in a month, the calendar

is actually a way of *counting days*. You can help students with this idea:

Today is September 13. Thirteen days have already gone by in this month. If we start counting on 1, what number do you think we will end up on? Let's try it.

As you involve students in this way, they have another chance to see that numbers represent a quantity, in this case a number of days.

Missing Numbers or Mixed-Up Numbers Once students are familiar with the structure of the calendar and the sequence of numbers, you can play two games that involve removing and rearranging the dates. To play Missing Numbers, choose two or three dates on the monthly calendar and either remove or cover them. As students guess which numbers are missing, encourage them to explain their thinking and reasoning. Do they count from the number 1 or do they count on from another number? Do they know that 13 comes *after* 12 and *before* 14?

Mixed-Up Numbers is played by changing the position of numbers on the calendar so that some are out of order. Students then fix the calendar by pointing out which numbers are out of order.

Patterns on the Calendar

Looking for Patterns Some teachers like to point out patterns on the calendar. The repeating sequence of the days of the week and the months of the year are patterns that help students explore the cyclical nature of time. Many students quickly recognize the sequence of numbers 1 to 30 or 31, and some even recognize another important pattern on the calendar: that the columns increase by 7. However, in order to maintain the focus on the calendar as a tool for keeping track of time, we recommend using the Calendar routine only to note patterns that exist within the structure of the calendar and the sequence of days and numbers. The familiar activity of adding pictures or shapes to form repeating patterns can be better done in another routine, Patterns on the Pocket Chart.

Today's Question

Collecting, representing, and interpreting information are ongoing activities in our daily lives. In today's world, organizing and interpreting data are vital to understanding events and making decisions based on this understanding. Because young students are natural collectors of materials and information, working with data builds on their natural curiosity about the world and people.

Today's Question offers students regular opportunities to collect information, record it on a class chart, and then discuss what it means. While engaged in this data collection and analysis, students are also counting real, meaningful quantities (How many of us have a pet?) and comparing quantities that are significant to them (Are there more girls in our class or more boys?). When working with questions that have only two responses, students explore part-whole relationships as they consider the total number of answers from the class and how that amount is broken into two parts.

Today's Question is introduced in the first unit of the kindergarten curriculum, *Mathematical Thinking in Kindergarten.* The basic routine is described here, followed by variations. Plan to use this routine throughout the school year on a weekly basis, or whenever a suitable and interesting question arises in your classroom.

Materials and Preparation

Prepare a chart for collecting students' responses to Today's Question. If you plan to use this routine frequently, either laminate a chart so that students can respond with wipe-off markers, or set up a blank chart on 11-by-17-inch paper and make multiple photocopies. The drawback of a laminated wipe-off chart is that you cannot save the information collected; with multiple charts, you can look back at data you have collected earlier or compare data from previous questions.

Make a section across the top of the chart, large enough to write the words *Today's Question* followed by the actual question being asked.

Mark the rest of the chart into two equal columns (later, you may want three columns). Leave enough space at the top of each column for the response choices, including words and possibly a sketch as a visual reminder.

Leave the bottom section (the largest part of the chart) blank for students to write their names to indicate their response. Your chart will look something like this:

Later in the year, you may want a chart with write-on lines in the bottom section to help students to compare numbers of responses in the two or three categories. Be sure to allow one line for each child in the class. Lines are also helpful guides if you collect data with "name pins," or clothespins marked on both sides with student names, as suggested for the Attendance routine (see illustration on p. 99).

Choosing Questions

Especially during the first half of the school year, try to choose questions with only two responses. With two categories of data, students are more likely to see the part-whole relationship between the number of responses in each category and the total number of students in the class.

As your students become familiar with the routine and with analyzing the data they collect, you may decide to add a third response category. This is useful for questions that might not always elicit a clear yes-or-no response, such as these:

Do you think it will rain? *(yes, no, maybe)*

Do you want to play outside today? *(yes, no, I'm not sure)*

Do you eat lunch at school? *(yes, no, sometimes)*

As you choose questions and set up the charts for this routine, consider the full range of responses and modify or drop the question if there seem to be too many possible answers. Later in the year, as students become familiar with this routine, you may want to involve them in organizing and choosing Today's Question.

Questions About the Class With Today's Question, students can collect information about a group of people and learn more about their classmates. For example:

Are you a boy or a girl?

Are you 5 or 6 years old?

Do you have a younger brother?

Do you have a pet?

Did you bring your lunch to school today?

Do you go to an after-school program?

Do you like ice cream?

Did you walk or ride to school this morning?

Some teachers avoid questions about potentially sensitive issues (Have you lost a tooth? Can you tie your shoes?), while other use this routine to carefully raise some of these issues. Whichever you decide, it is best to avoid questions about material possessions (Does your family have a computer?).

Questions for Daily Decisions When you pose questions that involve students in making decisions about their classroom, they begin to see that they are collecting real data for a purpose. These data collection experiences underscore one of the main reasons for collecting data in the real world: to help people make decisions. For example:

Which book would you like me to read at story time? (Display two books.)

Would you prefer apples or grapes for snack?

Should we play on the playground or walk to the park today?

Questions for Curriculum Planning Some teachers use this routine to gather information that helps them plan the direction of a new curriculum topic or lesson. For example, you can learn about students' previous experiences and better prepare them before reading a particular story, meeting a special visitor, or going on a field trip, with questions like these:

Have you ever read or heard this story?

Have you ever been to the science museum?

Have you ever heard of George Washington?

For questions of this type, you might want to add a third possible response (*I'm not sure* or *I don't know*).

Discussing the Data

Data collection does not end with the creation of a representation or graph to show everyone's responses. In fact, much of the real work in data analysis begins after the data has been organized and represented. Each time students respond to Today's Question, it is important to discuss the results. Consider the following questions to promote data analysis in classroom discussions:

What do you think this graph is about?

What do you notice about this graph?

What can you tell about [the favorite part of our lunch] by looking at this graph?

If we went to another classroom, collected this same information, and made a graph, do you think that graph would look the same as or different from ours?

Graphs and other visual representations of the data are vehicles for communication. Thinking about what a graph represents or what it is communicating is a part of data analysis that even the youngest students can and should be doing.

Patterns on the Pocket Chart

Mathematics is sometimes called "the science of patterns." We often use the language of mathematics to describe and predict numerical or geometrical regularities. When young students examine patterns, they look for relationships among the pattern elements and explore how that information can be used to predict what comes next. The classroom routine Patterns on the Pocket Chart offers students repeated opportunities to describe, copy, extend, create, and make predictions about repeating patterns. The use of a 10-by-10 pocket chart to investigate patterns of color and shape builds a foundation for the later grades, when this same pocket chart will display the numbers 1 to 100 and students will investigate patterns in the arrangement of numbers.

This routine is introduced in the second unit of the kindergarten curriculum, *Pattern Trains and Hopscotch Paths*. The basic routine is described here, followed by variations for use throughout the school year on a weekly basis.

Materials and Preparation

For this routine you will need a pocket chart, such as the vinyl Hundred Number Wall Chart (with transparent pockets and removable number cards). You will also need 2-inch squares of construction paper of different colors, a set of color tiles (ideally, the colors of the paper squares will match the tiles), a set of 20–30 What Comes Next? cards. These cards, with a large question mark in the center, are cut slightly larger than 2 inches so they will cover the colored squares. A blackline master for these cards is provided in the unit *Pattern Trains and Hopscotch Paths*. You can easily make your own cards with tagboard and a marking pen.

For the variation Shapes, Shells, and Such, you can use math manipulatives such as pattern blocks and interlocking cubes, picture or shape cards, or collections of small objects, such as buttons, keys, or shells. The only limitation is the size of the pockets on your chart.

What Comes Next?

Before introducing this activity, arrange an a-b repeating pattern in the first row of the pocket chart using ten paper squares in two colors of your choice. Beginning with the fifth position, cover each colored square with a What Comes Next? (question mark) card.

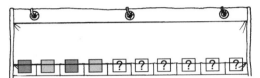

Gather students where the pocket chart is clearly visible and they have a place to work with color tiles, either on the floor or at tables.

Begin by asking students what they notice about the chart. Some may comment on the structure of the chart, some on the two-color pattern, and others may notice the question marks. Explain that each time they see one of these question marks, they should think "What comes next?" and decide what color might be under that card.

Provide each pair with a small cup of color tiles that match the paper squares. Ask students to build the first part of the pattern with color tiles and then predict what color comes next.

Who can predict, or guess, what color is hidden under each question mark on our chart? Use the tiles in your cup to show me what color would come next. How do you know?

Now, with your partner, see if you can make this pattern longer, using the tiles in your cup. Stop when your pattern has ten tiles.

When everyone has made a longer pattern, "read" the pattern together as a whole class. Verbalizing the pattern they are considering often helps students internalize it, recognize any errors in the pattern, and determine what comes next.

This basic activity can be done quickly, especially if students do not build the pattern with tiles. Many teachers integrate this routine into their group meeting time on a regular basis, making one or two patterns on the pocket chart and asking students to predict what comes next.

Initially, use only two colors or two variables in the patterns. In addition to a-b (for example, blue-green) repeating patterns, build two-color patterns such as a-a-b (blue-blue-green), a-b-b (blue-green-green), or a-a-b-b (blue-blue-green-green).

Variations

Making Longer Patterns When students are familiar with the basic activity, they can investigate what happens to an a-b pattern when it "wraps around" and continues to the next line. If the pattern continues in a left-to-right progression, the pattern that emerges is the same one older students see when they investigate the patterns of odd and even numbers on the 100 chart.

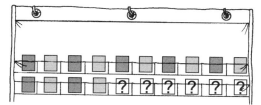

Shapes, Shells, and Such Color is just one variable for patterns; others can be made using a wide variety of materials and pictures.

shell, shell, button, shell, shell, button

triangle, square, triangle, square

♡ ☾ ♡ ☾ ♡ ☾

⇧ ⇩ ⇩ ⇧ ⇩ ⇩ ⇧ ⇩ ⇩

Picture cards, sometimes used by kindergarten teachers to make patterns on the calendar, make great patterns on the pocket chart without the distraction of the calendar elements.

What Comes *Here*? Predicting what comes next is an important idea in learning about patterns. Also important is being able to look ahead and predict what comes *here?* even further down the line. Instead of asking for the *next* color in a pattern sequence, point to a pocket three or four squares along and ask students to predict the

color under that question mark. As you collect responses, ask students to explain how they predicted that color.

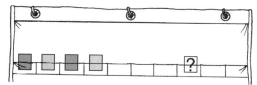

Border Patterns Explore a repeating pattern that extends around the entire outer edge of the pocket chart. Begin by filling the top row of the chart and asking what color would come next if this pattern turned the corner and went down the right side of the chart. Continue adding squares to finish the border. Every few days, begin a new pattern and ask students to help you complete the border. Start with a-b patterns. Gradually vary the pattern type, but continue to use only two colors, trying patterns such as a-a-b, a-b-b, a-a-b-b, or a-a-b-a. Ask students to notice which types make a continuous pattern all around the border and which do not.

With any border pattern, you can include a few What Comes Next? cards and ask students to predict the color of a particular pocket.

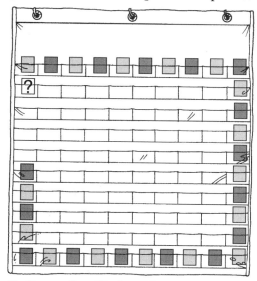

Patterns for Choice Time Hang the pocket chart where students can reach it. During free time or Choice Time, two or three students can work together to make their own pattern on the pocket chart, using colored paper squares or color tiles.

It is likely that more students with limited English proficiency will be enrolled in kindergarten than any other grade. Moreover, many will be at the earliest stages of language acquisition. By correctly identifying a student's current level of English, you can create appropriate stimuli to ensure successful communication when presenting activities from *Investigations*.

The four stages of language acquisition are characterized as follows:

- **Preproduction** Students do not speak the language at this stage; they are dependent upon modeling, visual aids, and context clues to obtain meaning.

- **Early production** Students begin to produce isolated words in response to comprehensible questions. Responses are usually *yes*, *no*, or other single-word answers.

- **Speech emergence** Students now have a limited vocabulary and can respond in short phrases or sentences. Grammatical errors are common.

- **Intermediate fluency** Students can engage in conversation, producing full sentences.

You need to be aware of these four levels of proficiency while applying the following tips. The goal is always to ensure that students with limited English proficiency develop the same understandings as their English-speaking peers as they participate in this unit.

Tips for Small-Group Work Whenever possible, pair students with the same linguistic background and encourage them to complete the task in their native language. Students are more likely to have a successful exchange of ideas when they speak the same language. In other situations, teach all students how to make their communications comprehensible. For example, encourage students to point to objects they are discussing.

Tips for Whole-Class Activities To keep whole-group discussions comprehensible, draw simple sketches or diagrams on the board to illustrate key words; point to objects being discussed; use contrasting examples to help explain the attribute under discussion; model all directions; choose students to model activities or act out scenarios.

Tips for Observing the Students Assessment in the kindergarten units is based on your observations of students as they work, either independently or in groups. At times you will intervene by asking questions to help you evaluate a student's understanding. When questioning students, it is crucial not to misinterpret responses that are incomplete simply because of linguistic difficulties.

In many cases, students may understand the mathematical concept being asked about but not be able to articulate their thoughts in English. You need to formulate questions that allow students to respond at their stage of language acquisition in a way that indicates their mathematical understanding.

For example, this unit includes this suggestion for observing the class: "How do students describe the materials (e.g., pattern blocks)? Do they refer to them by shape? color? size?" When you are observing students at the speech-emergence and intermediate-fluency stages of acquisition, you will likely hear words of shape, color, and size spoken. However, students at earlier stages will probably not use the English terms. Therefore, you need to base your assessment on less-verbal indicators.

With students at the preproduction stage, for example, consider an alternative that calls for a nonverbal response: "Can the students show you a pattern block shape that is the same as one you point to?" With students at the early-production stage, you might look for single-word responses: "Can students tell you how many sides a particular pattern block has?"

As you observe the students working, keep in mind which guidelines are appropriate for students at the different stages of language acquisition. Following is a categorization of typical questions from this unit.

Questions appropriate for students at the prepro-duction stage:

- How do students use the pattern blocks? Do they lay the blocks flat to make designs or pictures? Do they stand them on edge or build vertically with them? Do they stack them?

- Do they have a sense that pairs or combinations of pattern blocks can be substituted for other blocks? For example, do they substitute two trapezoids for a hexagon, or two triangles for a blue rhombus?

- Do students use the color tiles to make repeating patterns (red, blue, red, blue)?

- As students count the objects [in the Counting Jar], do they organize them in any way? Do they touch or move each item as they count it? Do they double-check their count?

- How do students record the number they counted in the jar? Do they use pictures to repre-sent the objects? Do they use numbers? Do they have a strategy for figuring out how to write a particular number?

Questions appropriate for students at the early-production and early-speech-emergence stages:

- [When counting during the Attendance routine], do students know the sequence of number names?

- [During the Calendar routine], do students know the names of the days of the week?

- Do students label their cube constructions as representing familiar objects? (For example, "This is a TV," or "This is a tall building.")

Questions appropriate for students at the late-speech-emergence and intermediate-fluency stages:

- Do they talk about patterns in any way? How?

- How do students describe the tiles and their cre-ations? Do they refer to them by shape? by color?

- What features of the representation [of Today's Question] do students notice? Do they comment on relevant features of the data?

The following activities will help ensure that this unit is comprehensible to students who are acquiring English as a second language. The suggested approach is based on *The Natural Approach: Language Acquisition in the Classroom* by Stephen D. Krashen and Tracy D. Terrell (Alemany Press, 1983). The intent is for second-language learners to acquire new vocabulary in an active, meaningful context.

Note that *acquiring* a word is different from *learning* a word. Depending on their level of proficiency, students may be able to comprehend a word upon hearing it during an investigation, without being able to say it. Other students may be able to use the word orally, but not read or write it. The goal is to help students naturally acquire targeted vocabulary at their present level of proficiency.

name, how many

1. Set up two columns on the board. Label the first column with the number 1 and the second with the number 2.

2. Say your name aloud as you write it in column 1. Name another teacher known to the students and write it under your name.

3. Choose a student from the group and write his or her name in column 2. Repeat with another student's name.

4. Summarize what you have done thus far.

   I put my name, and [other teacher's] name, in column 1. But I put [student's] and [student's] name in column 2.

5. Select another student from the group and say his or her name aloud. Challenge the group to decide if you'll write that name under column 1 or 2.

6. Continue naming teacher and student names and asking students to decide which column the name should be written in.

7. Conclude by asking questions about the lists, beginning with "How many." Count with the group to answer the questions.

   How many teacher's names are in column 1?
   How many student's names are in column 2?
   How many boy's names are in column 2?

big, little, tiny, same, different

1. Show the students a selection of Geoblocks in three sizes (big, smaller, and the smallest 1-centimeter cube). Identify them as a big block, a little block, and a tiny block.

2. Hold up a duplicate of one of the blocks, and explain that it is the same as one of these. Hold up a triangular block that has no duplicate in this small collection. Explain that it is different from all the others.

3. Have students compare the blocks. Hold up two blocks at a time, asking questions that can be answered with one word or by pointing.

   Are these two blocks the same? Are they different?
   Which is the big block? Which of these blocks is small?
   Who can find a tiny block? Can you find a block that is the same as that tiny block?

color names

1. Show students small squares of construction paper in a wide variety of colors. Name each color as you lay the squares in a row on the table.

2. Make available a collection of colorful materials, including pattern blocks, interlocking cubes, color tiles, and teddy bear counters. Ask volunteers to take turns selecting an object and matching it, by color, to a square of paper. Ask that student or any student in the group to identify the color by name; if no one can, do so yourself.

3. When the materials have been sorted by color, call on students to take turns selecting an item of the color you name.

   Take something that is green.
   Take something that is orange.
   Take something that is blue.

4. For further practice, ask students to find objects in the classroom or items of clothing in the colors you name.

Blackline Masters

_____ , 19 _____

Dear Family,

As we start the year, we are working with a unit called *Mathematical Thinking in Kindergarten.* These are some of the activities we are going to be doing:

- We count the number of children in our class. We find the number who are present and absent. We also find how many are girls and how many are boys.

- We count the number of things in our Counting Jar. We record the total, using numbers or pictures to show how many. Then we create another set of things that has exactly the same amount as we found in the jar.

- We use a number line to become familiar with the numbers we are saying as we count aloud. When we want to record an amount, we copy these numbers.

- We use the calendar as a tool for keeping track of time and events. We also discover that it's another place we can visit the number sequence and practice counting numbers into the 20's.

- We work with pattern blocks and Geoblocks to make shapes, designs, buildings, and constructions with two- and three-dimensional shapes. We explore ways that different geometrical shapes fit together.

While our class is working on this unit, and throughout the year, you can help by staying in touch with your child's work. Here are a couple of things you can do while we start our unit in mathematics:

- Take advantage of any opportunities you might have to count with your child. Children learn to count by having many opportunities to see and hear other people count, and to count on their own. You can model counting out napkins or plates for the table, or crackers or fruit for snack. It would also be helpful to have a collection of objects your child can use to practice counting, such as beans, buttons, or pennies.

- Help your child explore your use of the calendar at home. When you write an appointment or a family event on your calendar, or when you use the calendar. to find out how many days until your trip, talk with your child about what you are doing. Explain how and why you are using a calendar. You might also point out examples of calendars when you see them.

We are looking forward to an exciting year as we create a mathematical community in our classroom.

Sincerely,

PATTERN BLOCK CUTOUTS (page 1 of 6)

Duplicate these hexagons on yellow paper and cut apart.

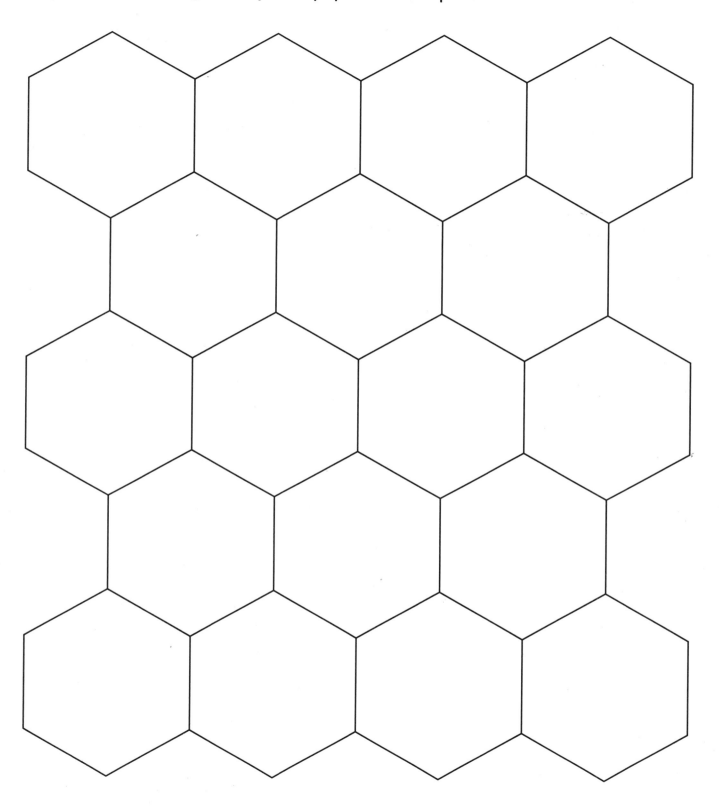

© Dale Seymour Publications®

Duplicate these trapezoids on red paper and cut apart.

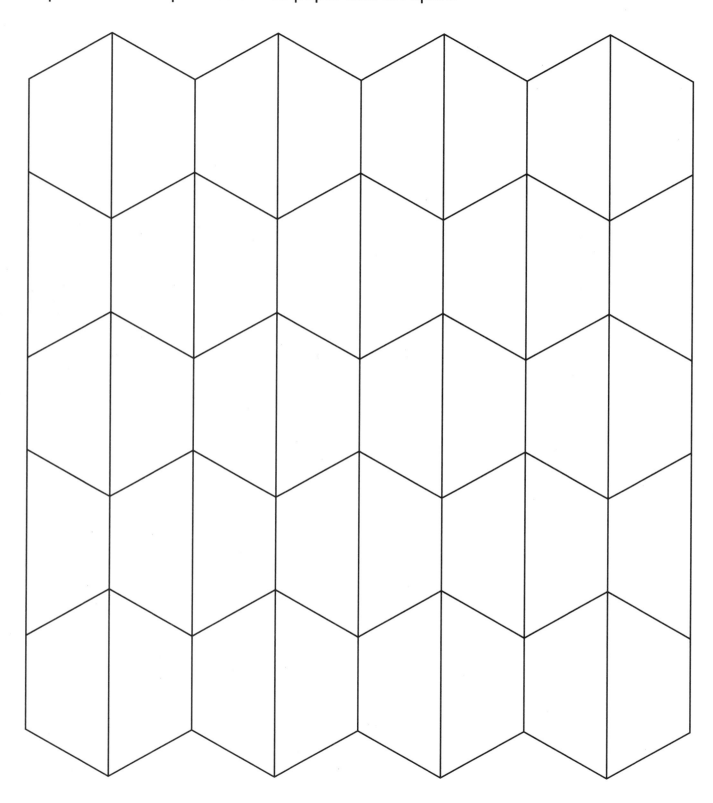

© Dale Seymour Publications®

Duplicate these triangles on green paper and cut apart.

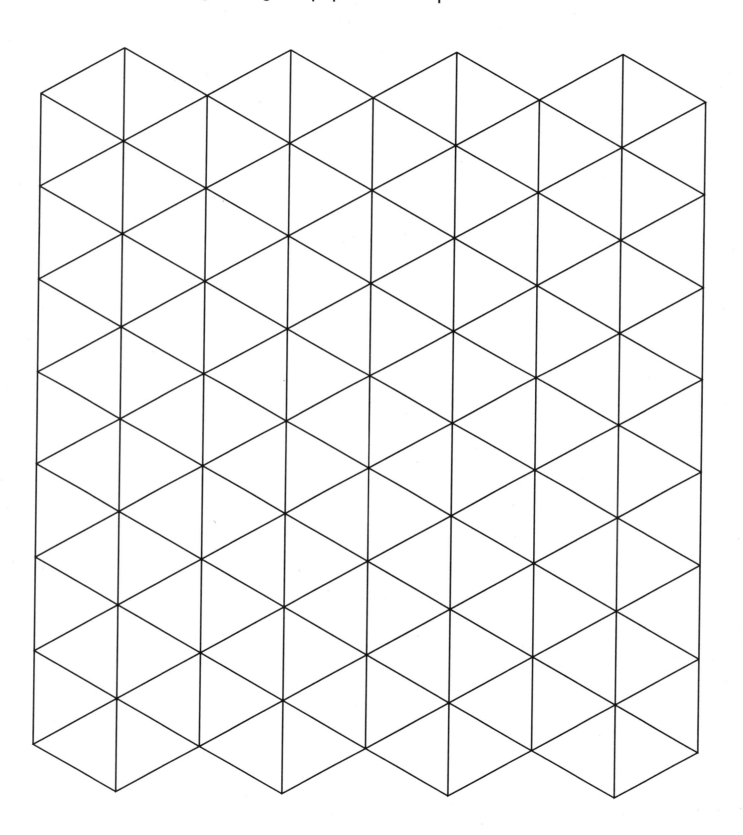

© Dale Seymour Publications®

83

Duplicate these squares on orange paper and cut apart.

© Dale Seymour Publications®

Duplicate these rhombuses on blue paper and cut apart.

85

PATTERN BLOCK CUTOUTS (page 6 of 6)

Duplicate these rhombuses on tan paper and cut apart.

© Dale Seymour Publications®

General Resource
Mathematical Thinking in Kindergarten

ONE-INCH GRID PAPER

87

Choice Board art for
Exploring Color Tiles

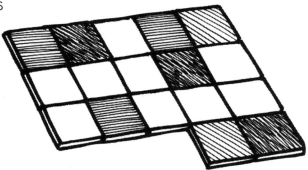

Choice Board art for
Exploring Pattern Blocks

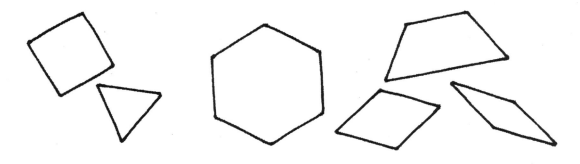

Choice Board art for
Exploring Geoblocks

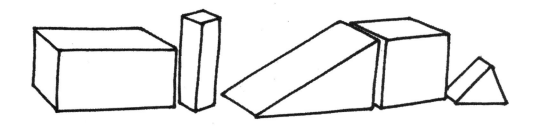

© Dale Seymour Publications®

Choice Board art for
Counting Jar

Choice Board art for
Exploring Interlocking Cubes